Acoustic Guitar Portraits

Duets for Two Acoustic Guitars

Online Audio

To Access the Online Audio Recording Go To:
WWW.MELBAY.COM/WBM03EB

WILLIAM
BAY **MUSIC**

WWW.MELBAY.COM

Forward

Acoustic Guitar Portraits is a collection of scores from my recording of the same name. The music reflects a rich variety of musical styles and is original. The rhythms are contemporary and the harmonies are lush. The duos feature an intricate dialogue between the two acoustic guitars. It has been my goal to present performance or concert material for the plectrum (flatpick) guitar. These compositions were written with that in mind.

Some of the scores call for a low A or B played on a 7 string guitar. These low pedal tones can easily be replaced by a low A or B as played on a 6 string guitar.

I would also recommend my sequel recording entitled **Christmas Guitar Portraits**. The scores for that duo collection are also available. Finally, I have an extensive recording of concert solos for plectrum guitar called **Guitar Images**. The scores for each of those original solos are available in the **Guitar Images** book.

William Bay

Contents

Composition	Page Number	Audio
Evensong	4	1
Lucia	8	2
Open Sea	16	3
Sea of Glass	20	4
Baad Times	26	5
Elegy for Two Guitars	34	6
Star in the Night	40	7
Canticle	46	8
Waves	52	9
Beatitude	58	10
Fading Dream	66	11
Hymn	70	12
Reflections	76	13
Signals	81	14
Twilight	86	15

Evensong

4

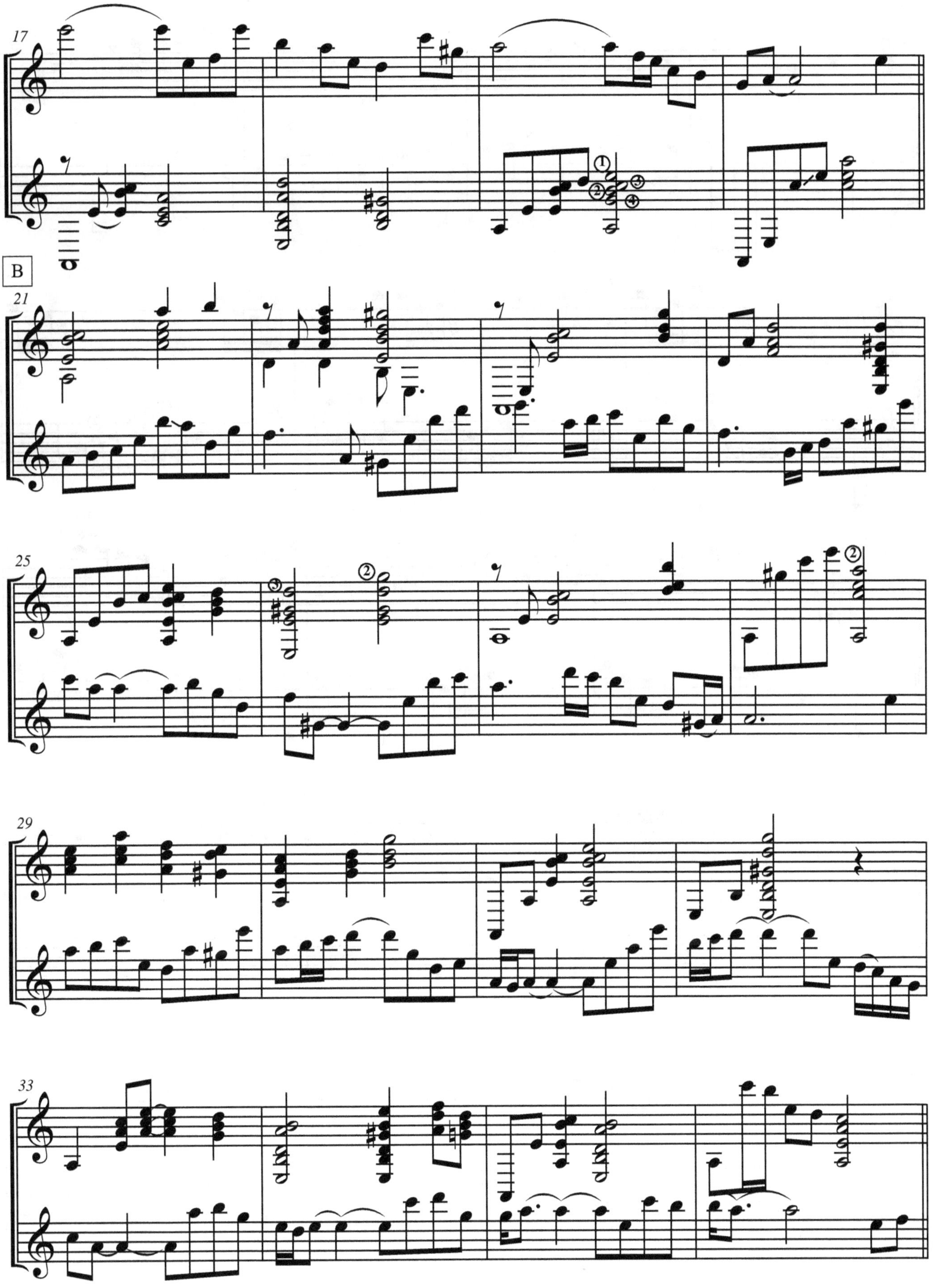
17
B
21
25
29
33

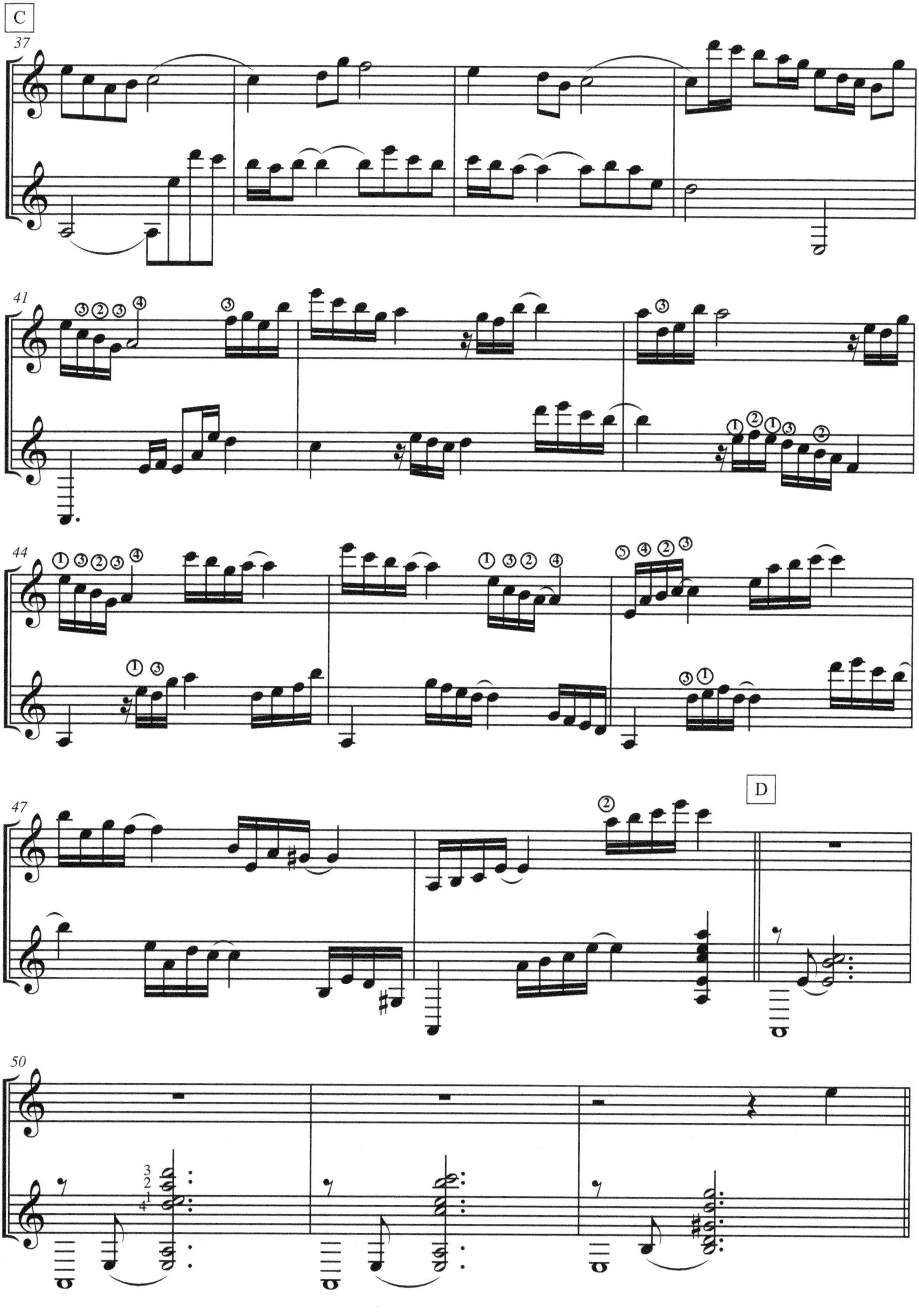
C
37
41
44
47
D
50

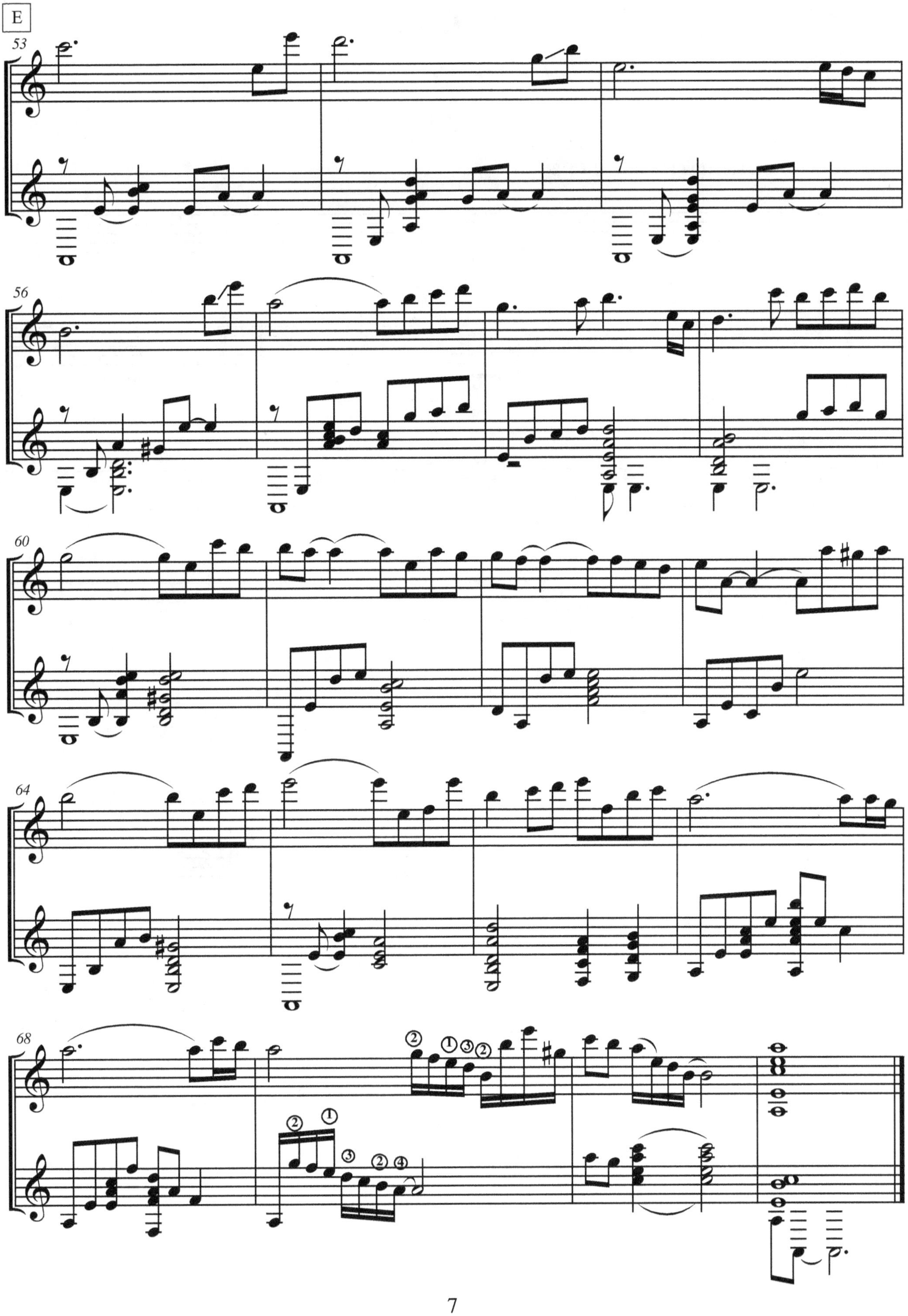
E
53
56
60
64
68

Lucia

Dropped D Tuning

William Bay

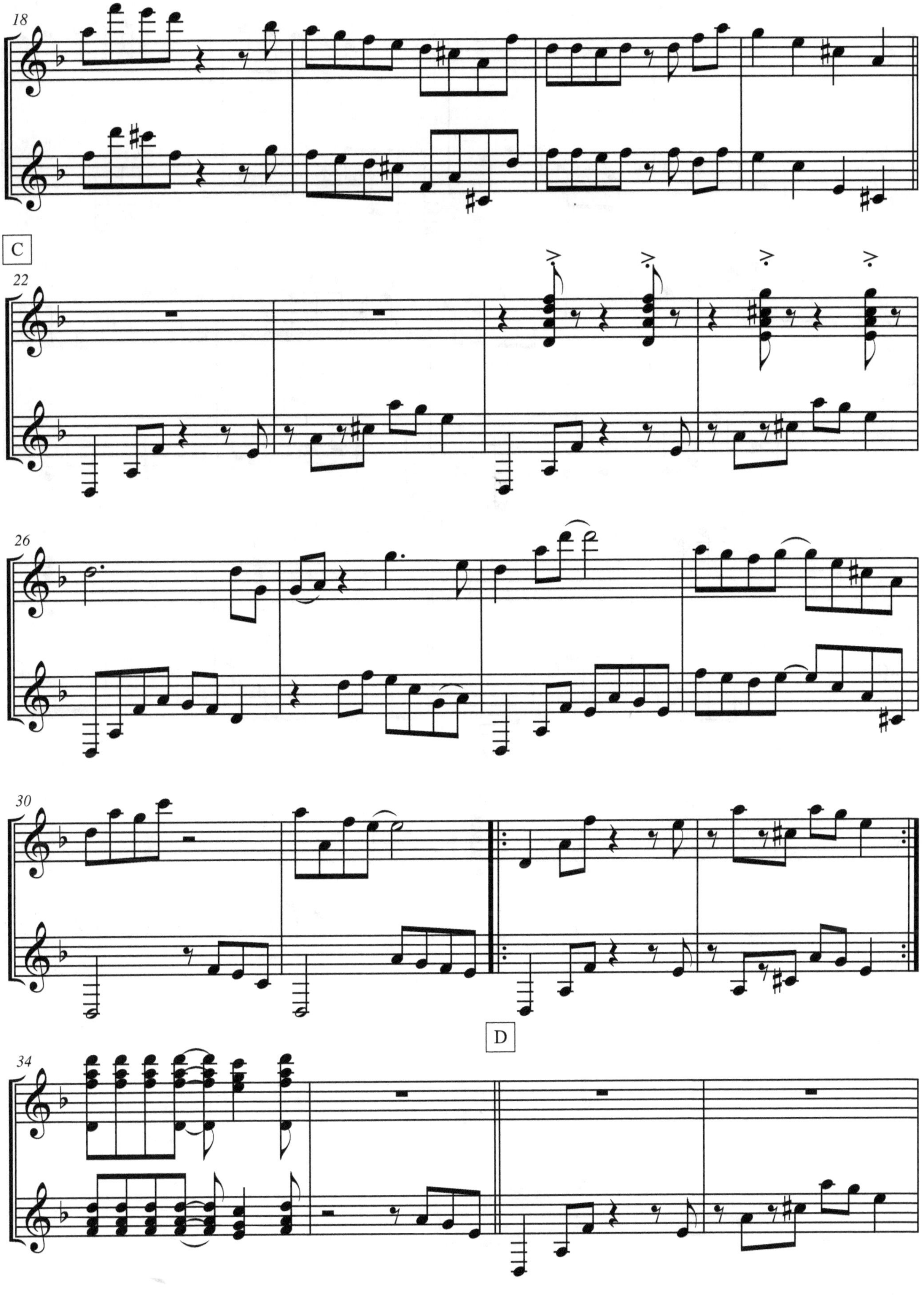
18
C
22
26
30
D
34

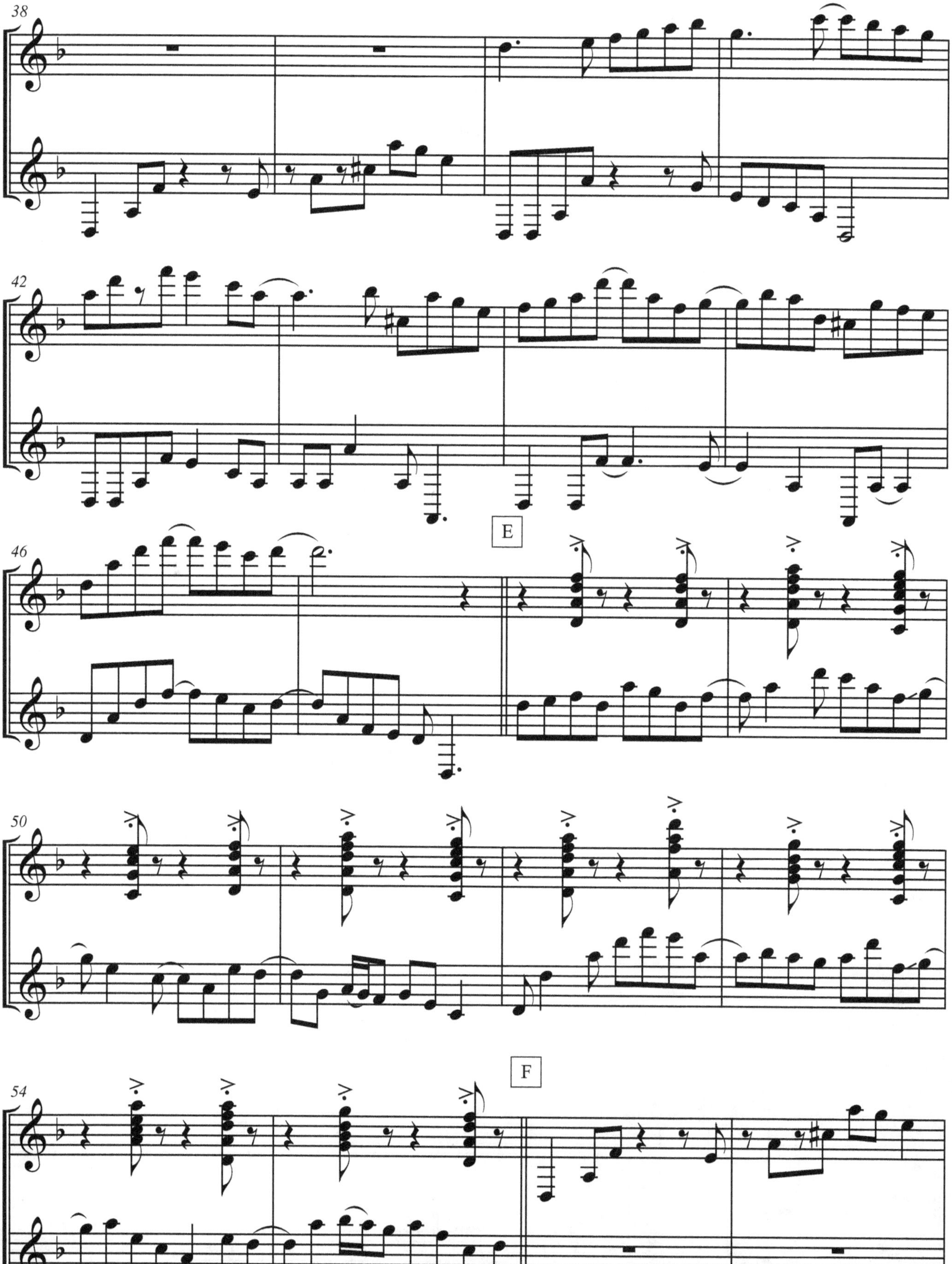
38
42
46
E
50
54
F

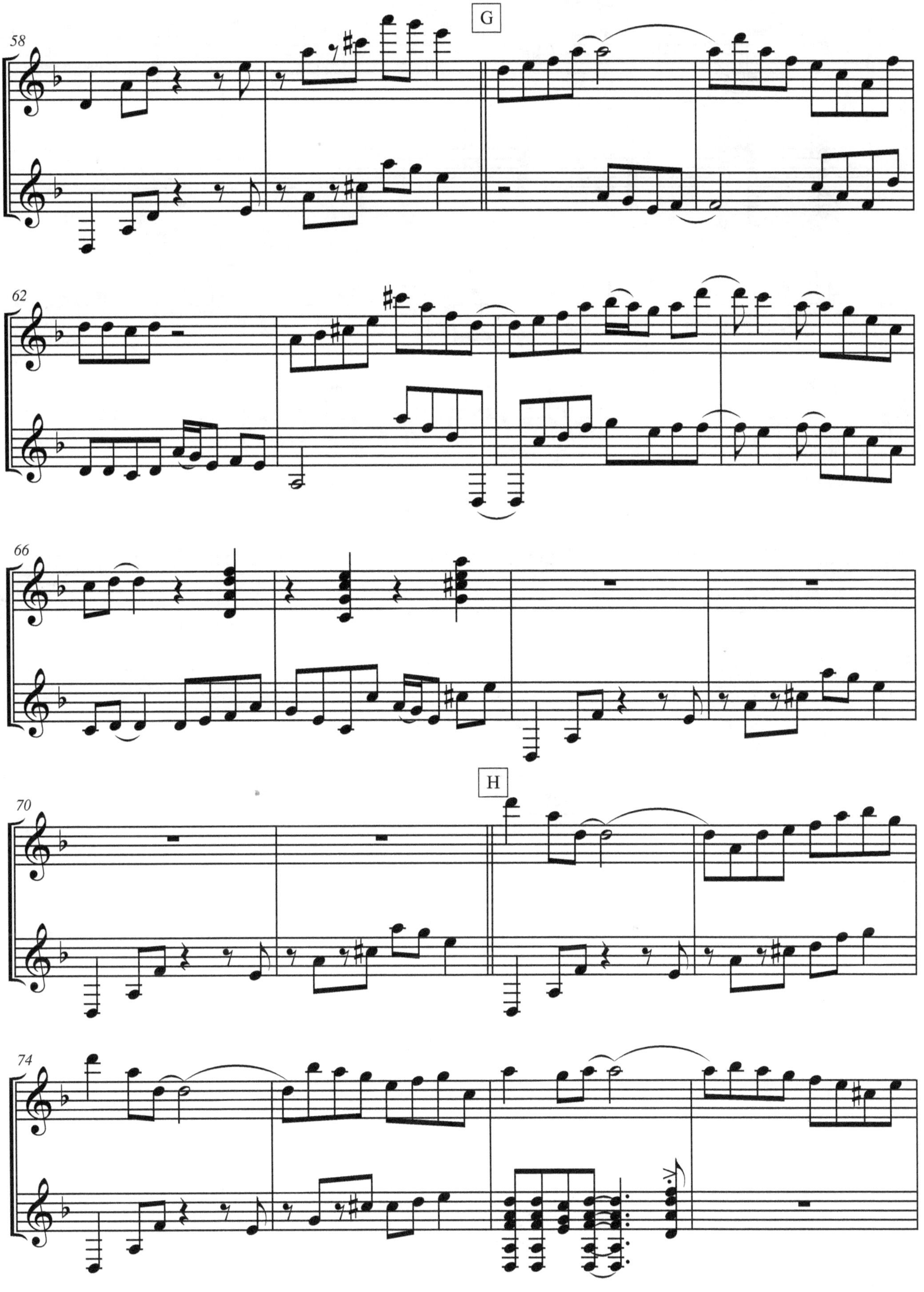
58
G
62
66
70
H
74

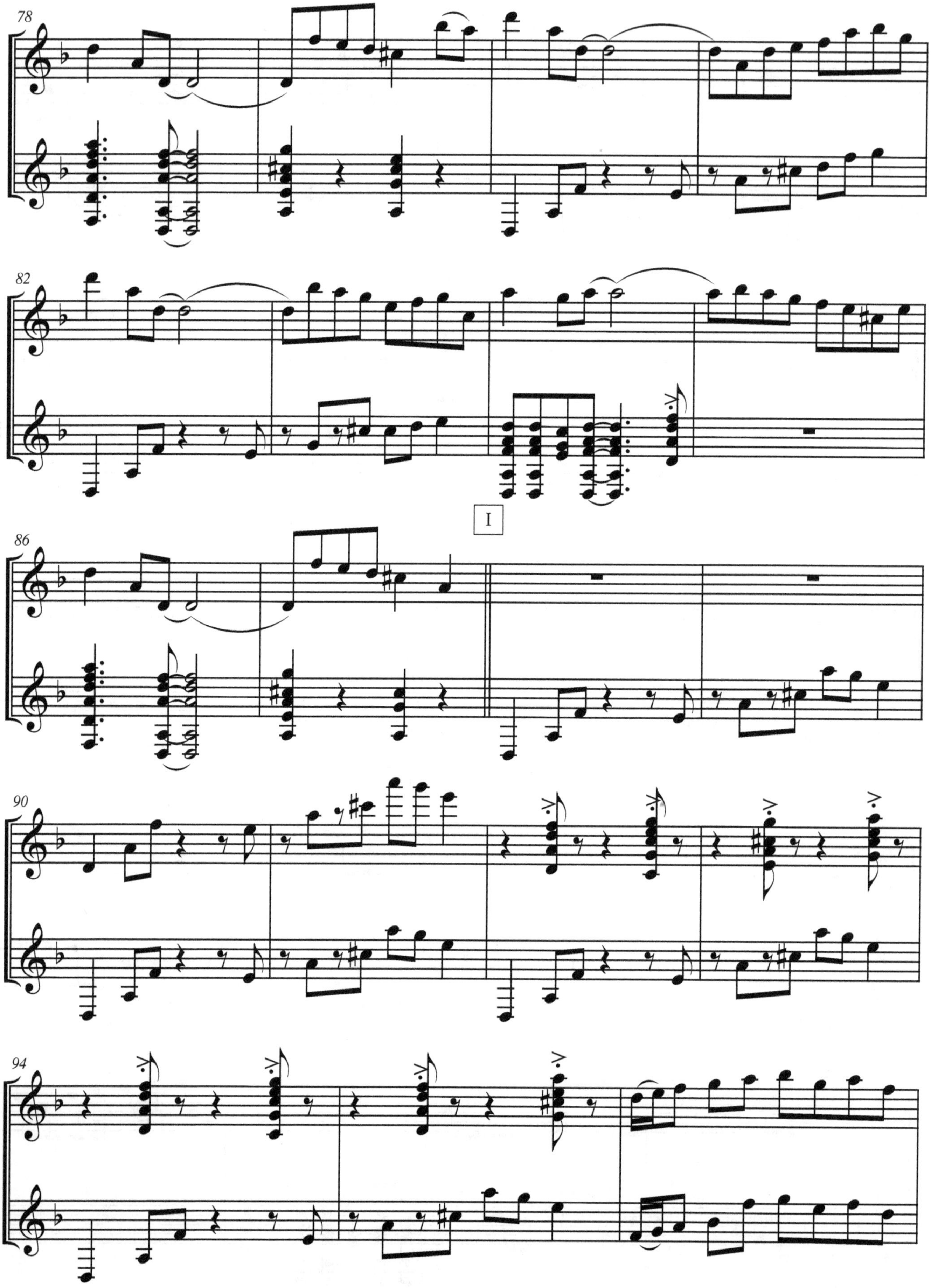
78
82
I
86
90
94

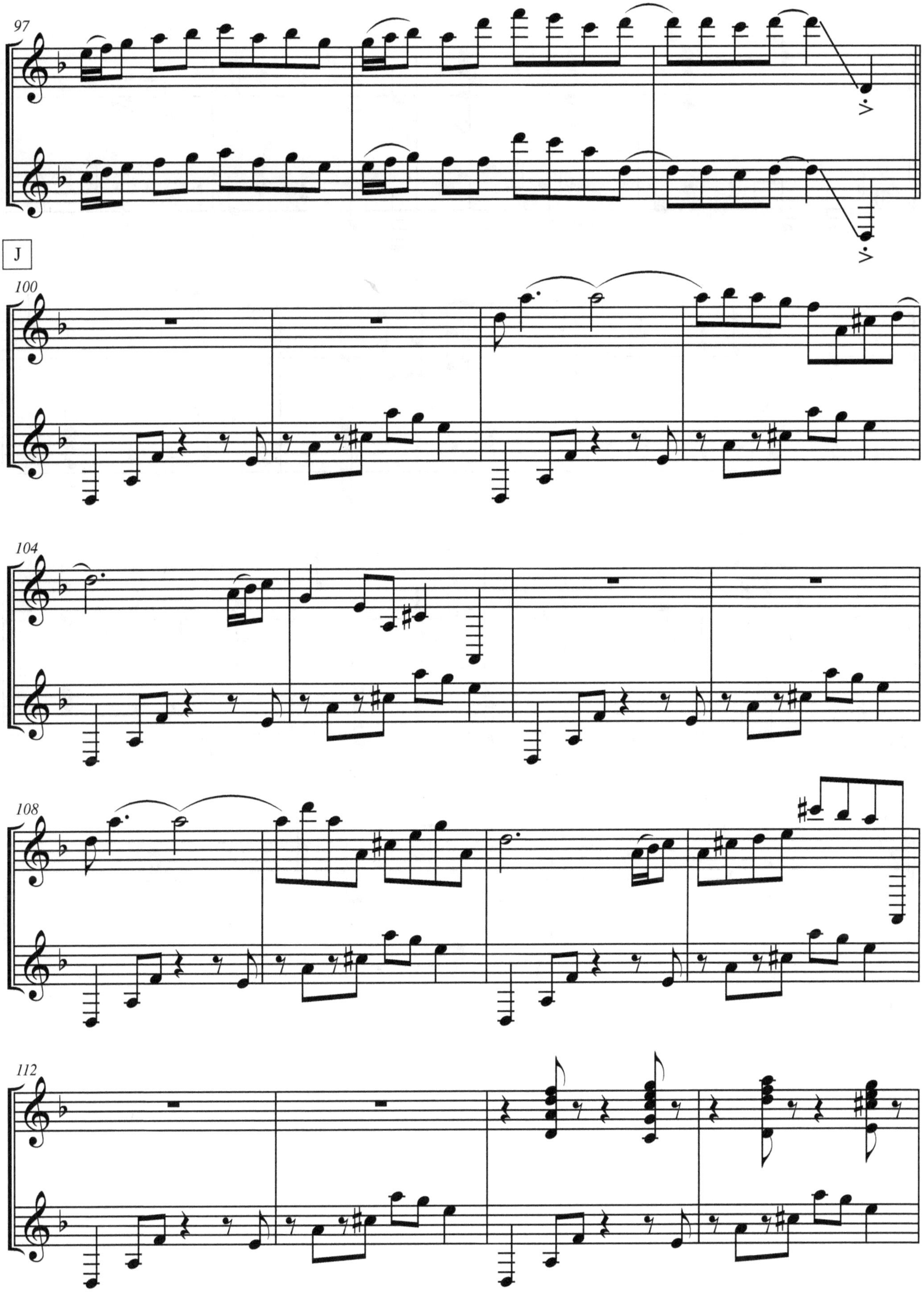
97
J
100
104
108
112

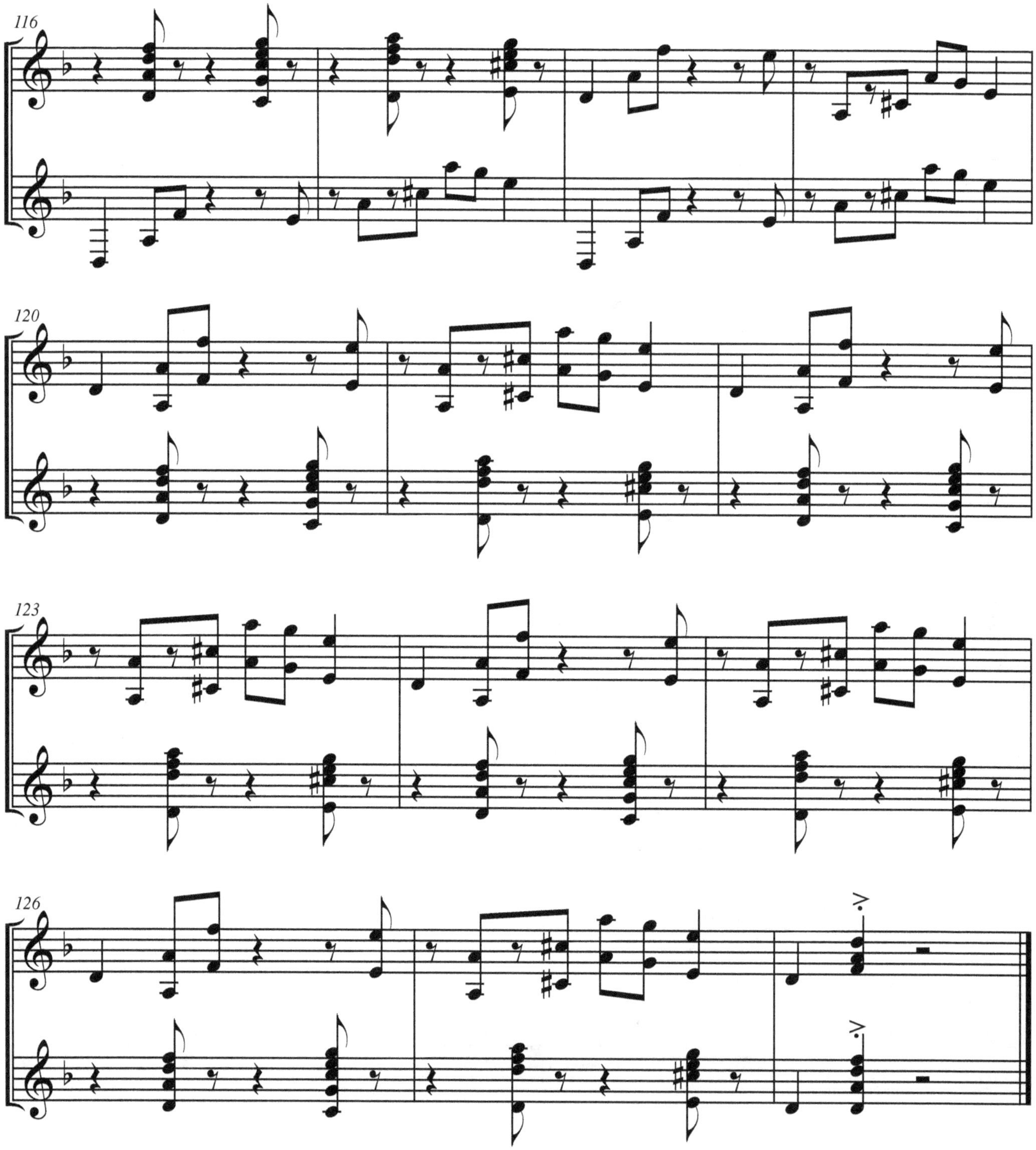
116
120
123
126

This page has been left blank
to avoid awkward page turns.

Open Sea

⑦ = A

Dropped D Tuning

William Bay

16

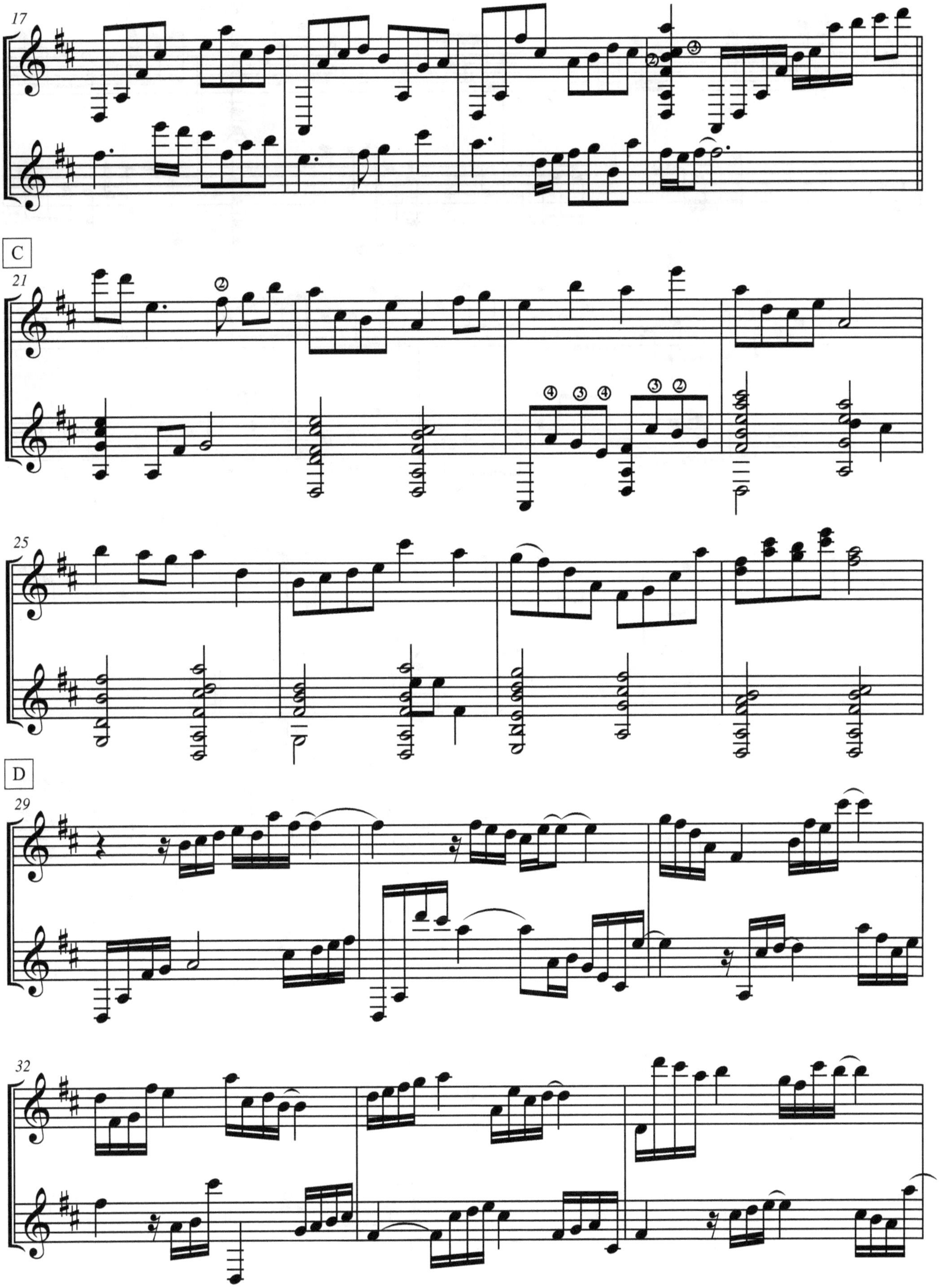
17
C
21
25
D
29
32

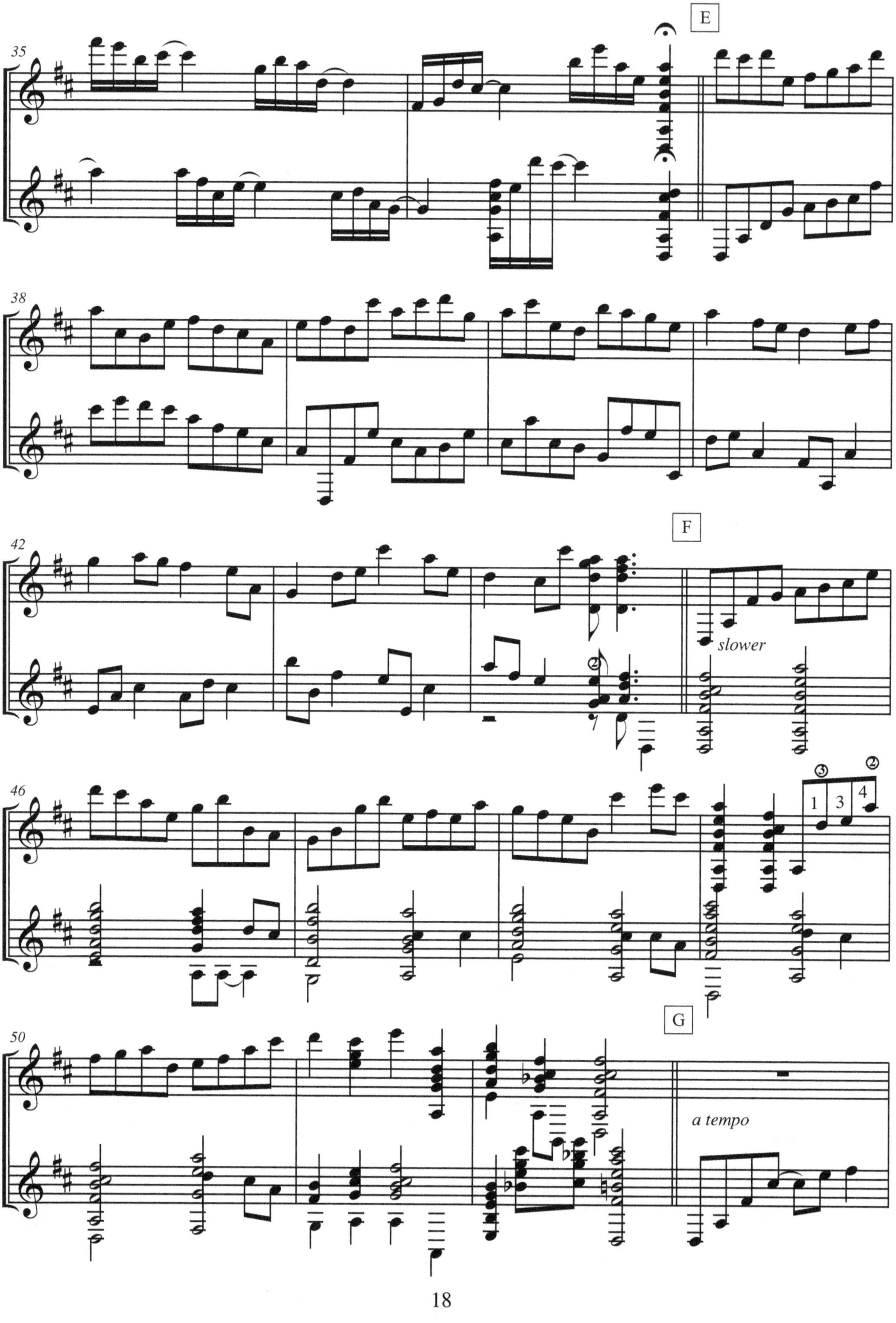

35
E
38
42
F
slower
46
50
G
a tempo

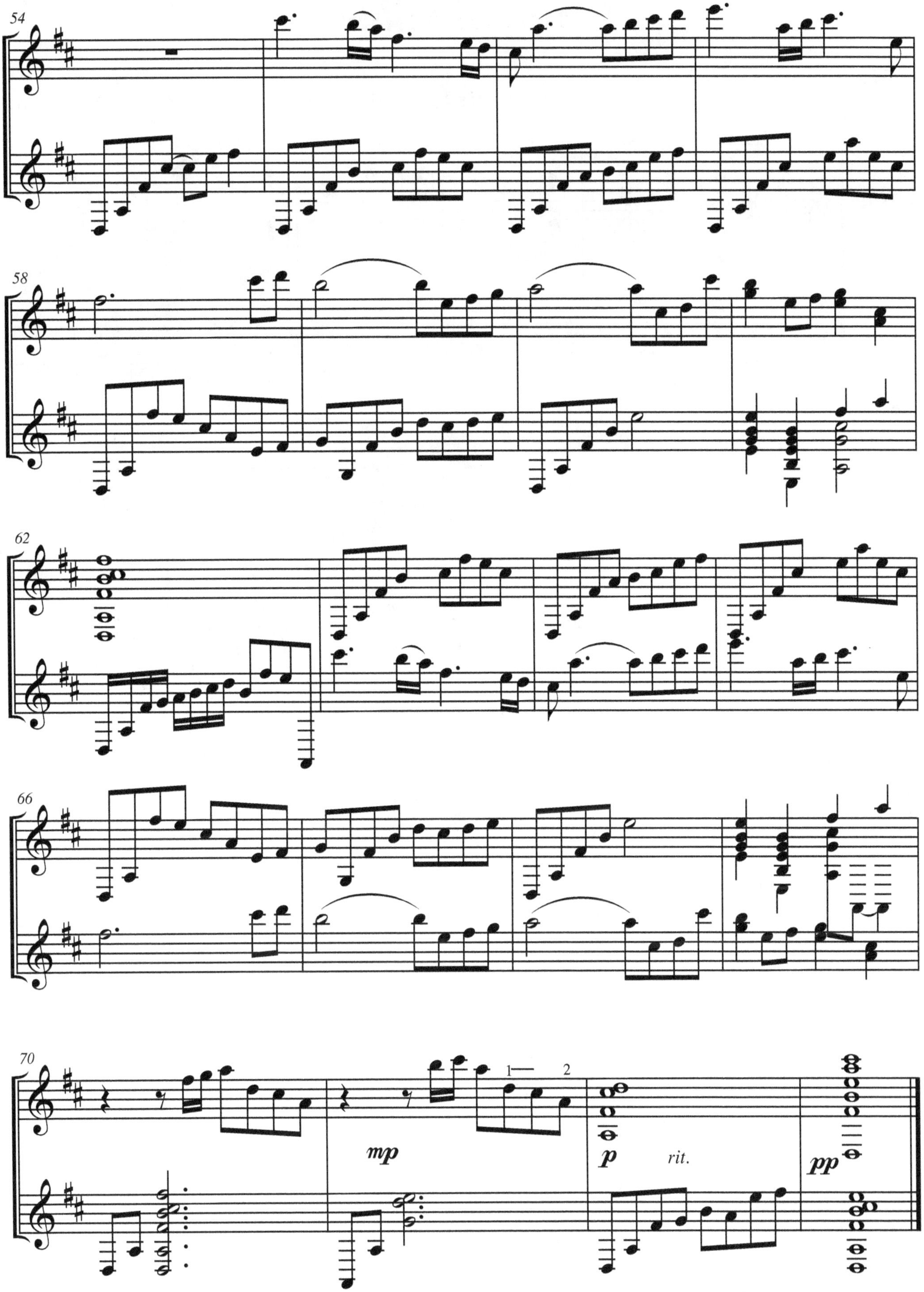
54
58
62
66
70
mp
p
rit.
pp

Sea of Glass

Dropped D Tuning

William Bay

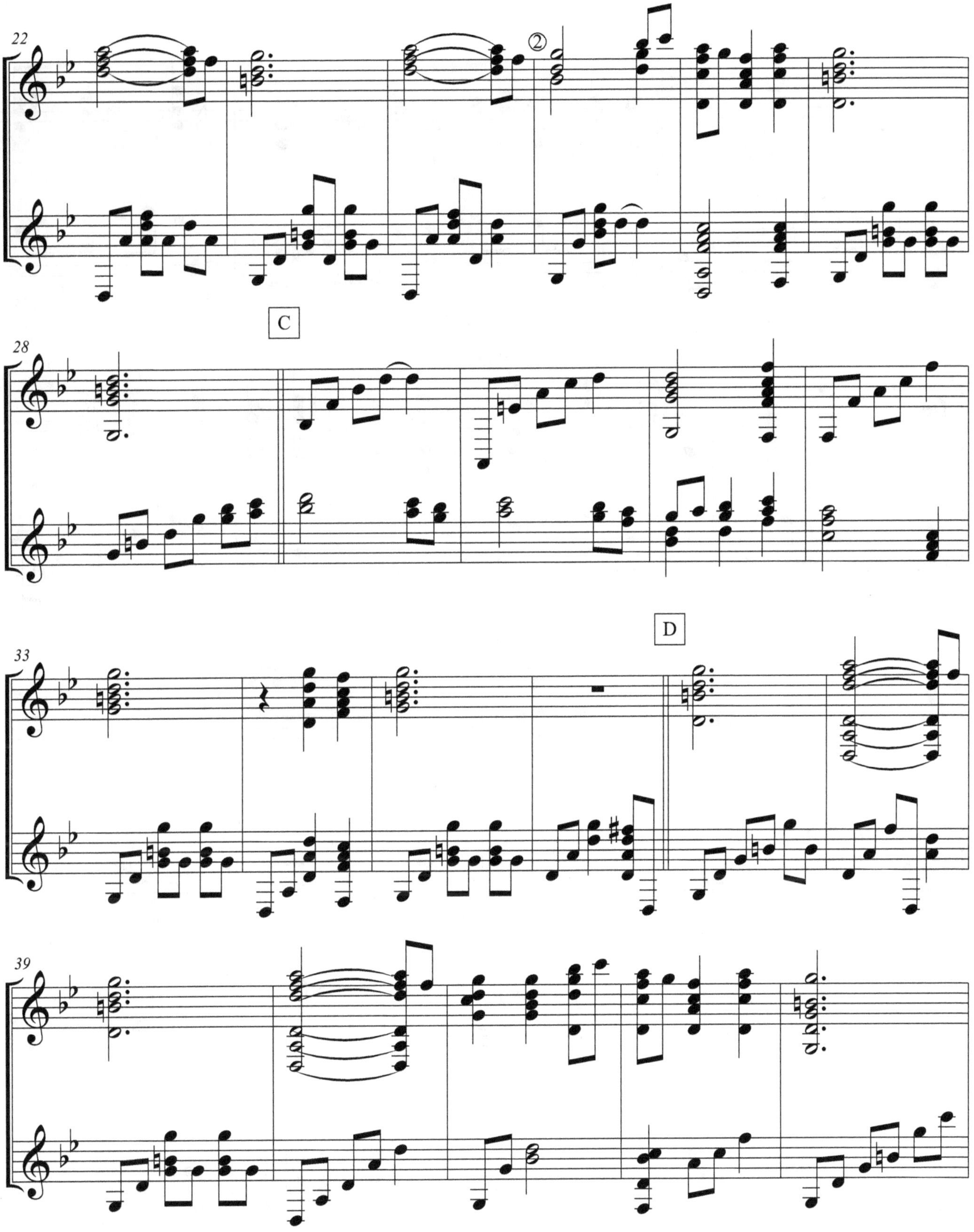
22
②
C
28
D
33
39

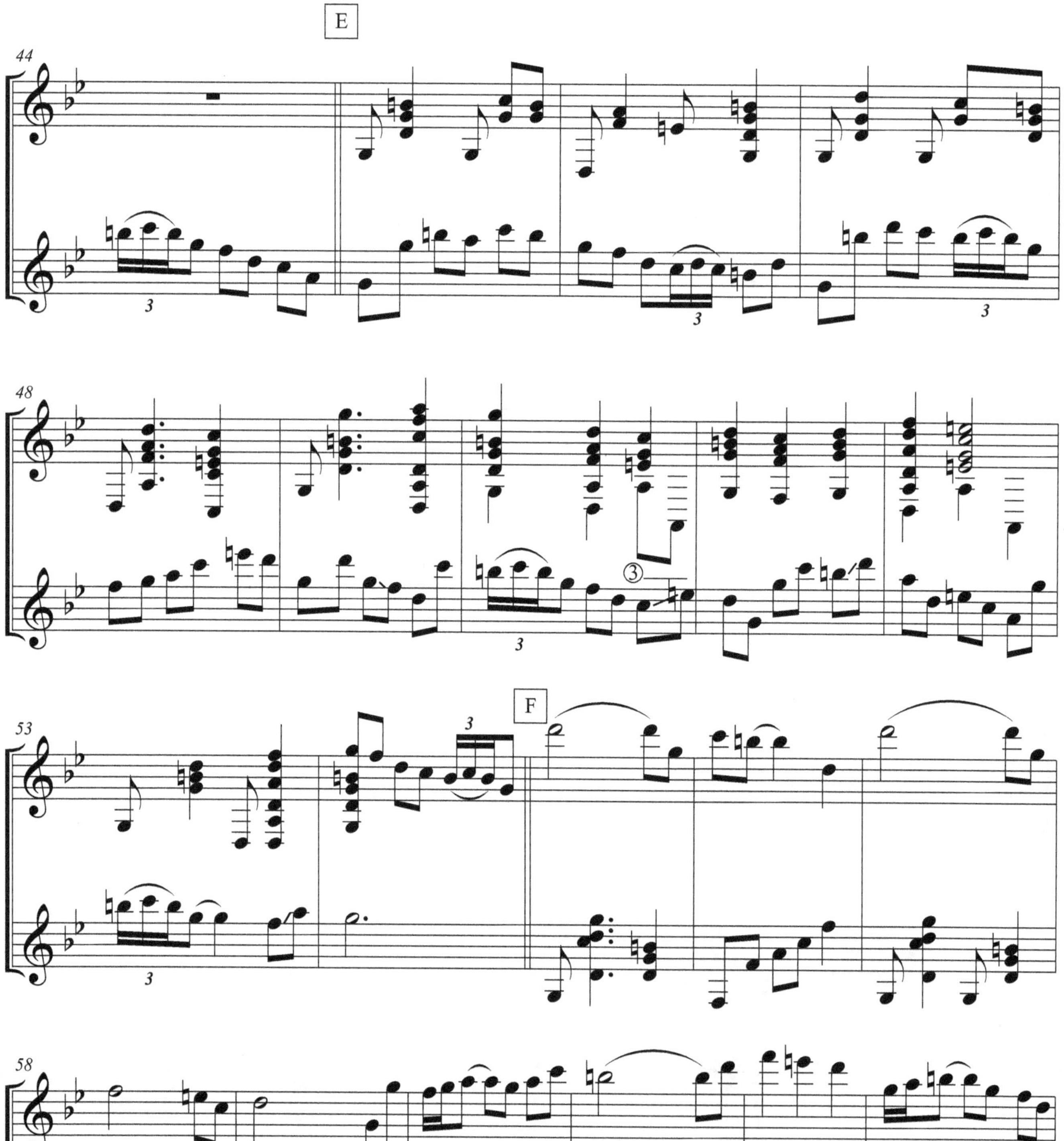
E
44
48
53
F
58

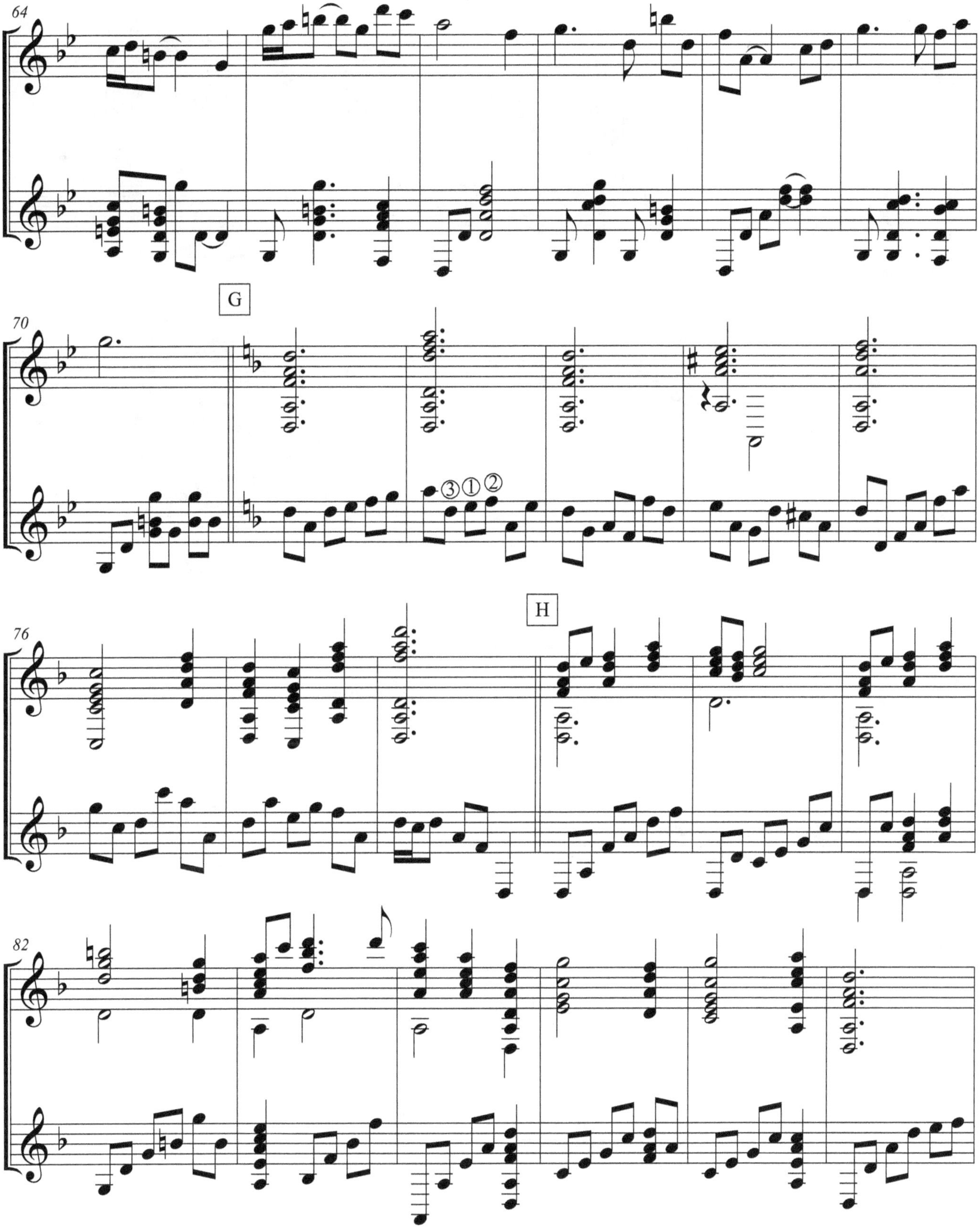
64
70
G
76
H
82
③①②

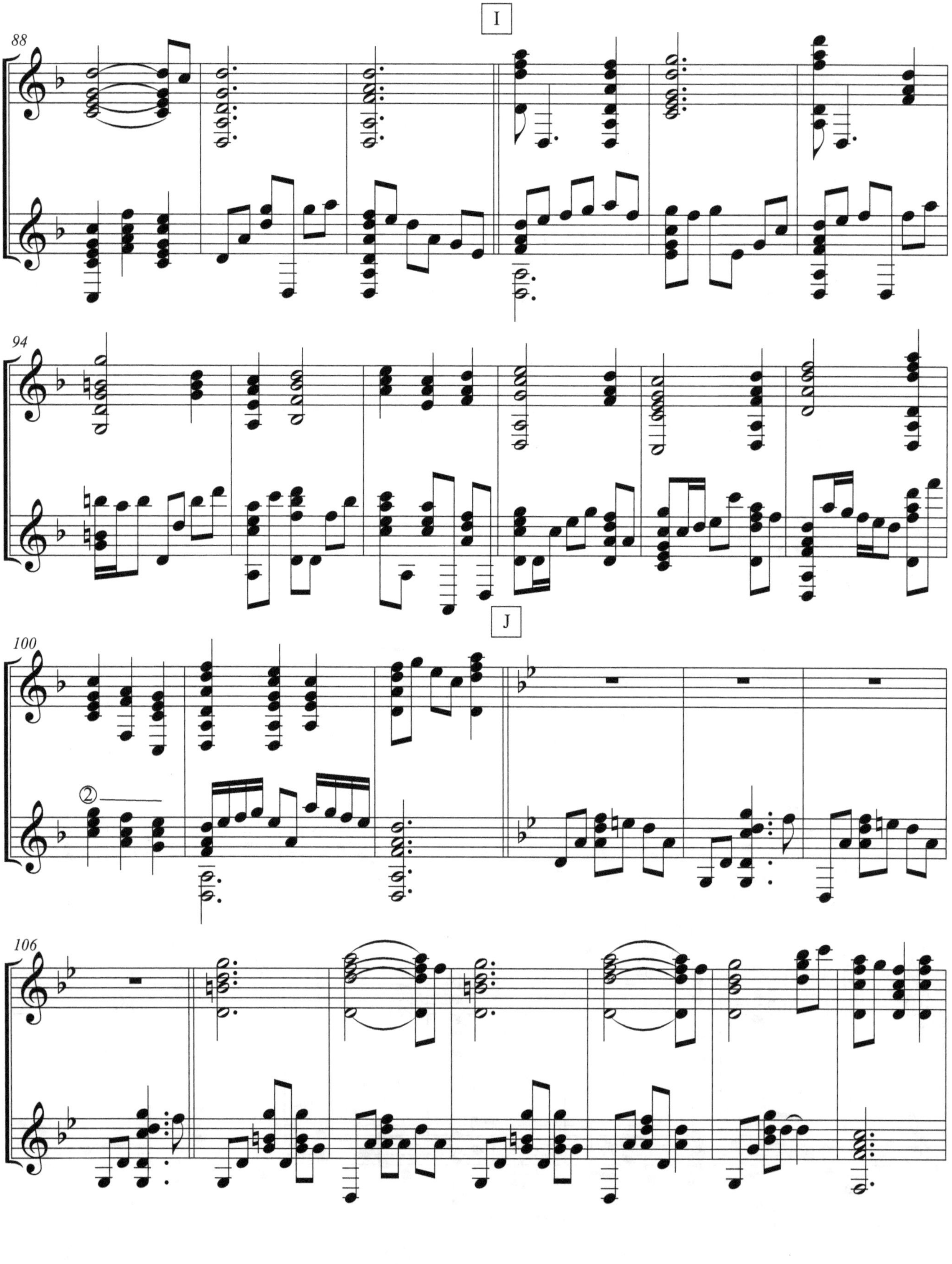
I
88
94
J
100
②
106

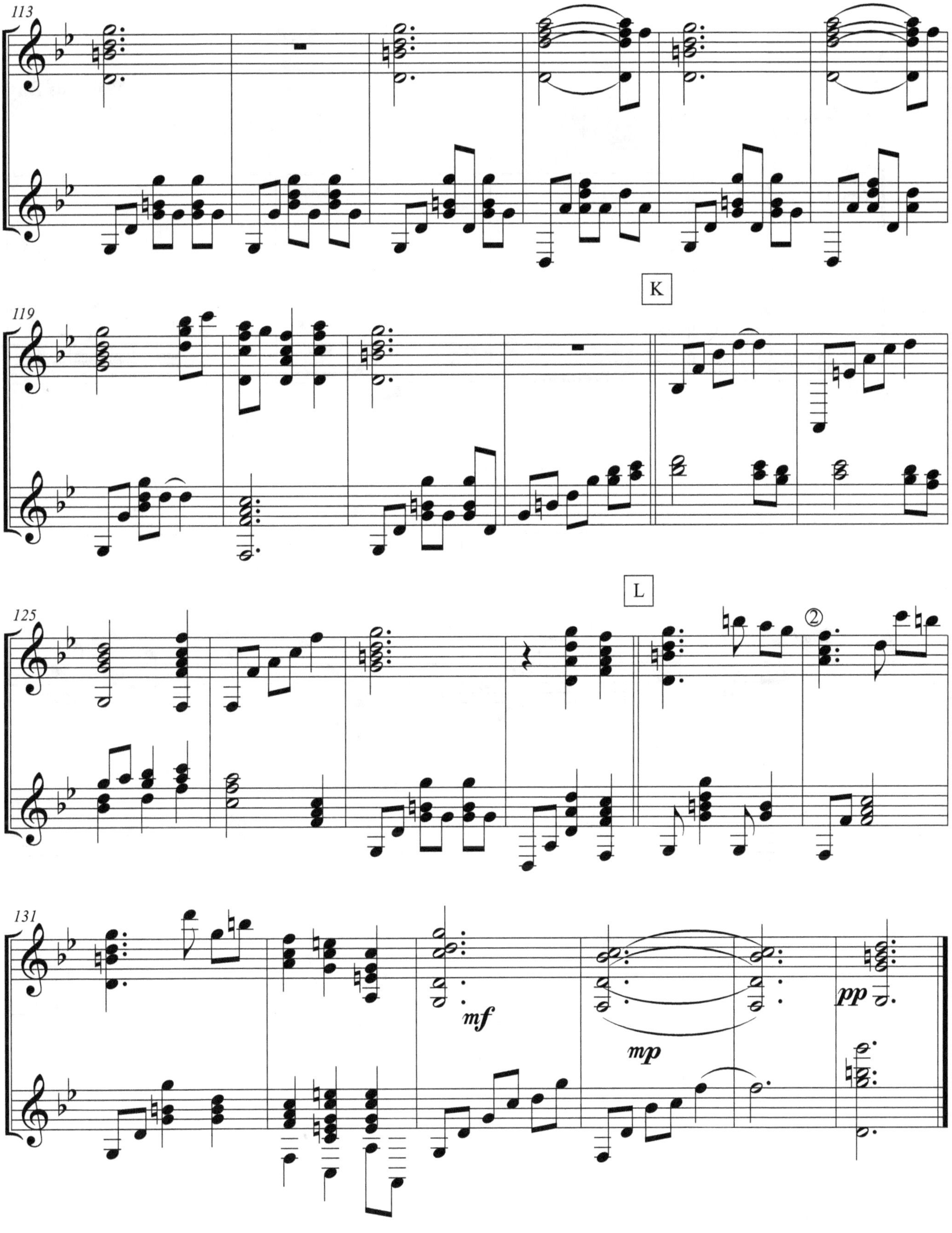
113
119
K
125
L
②
131
mf
mp
pp

Baad Times

⑦ = A

William Bay

Blues Feeling ♩ = 85   A

26

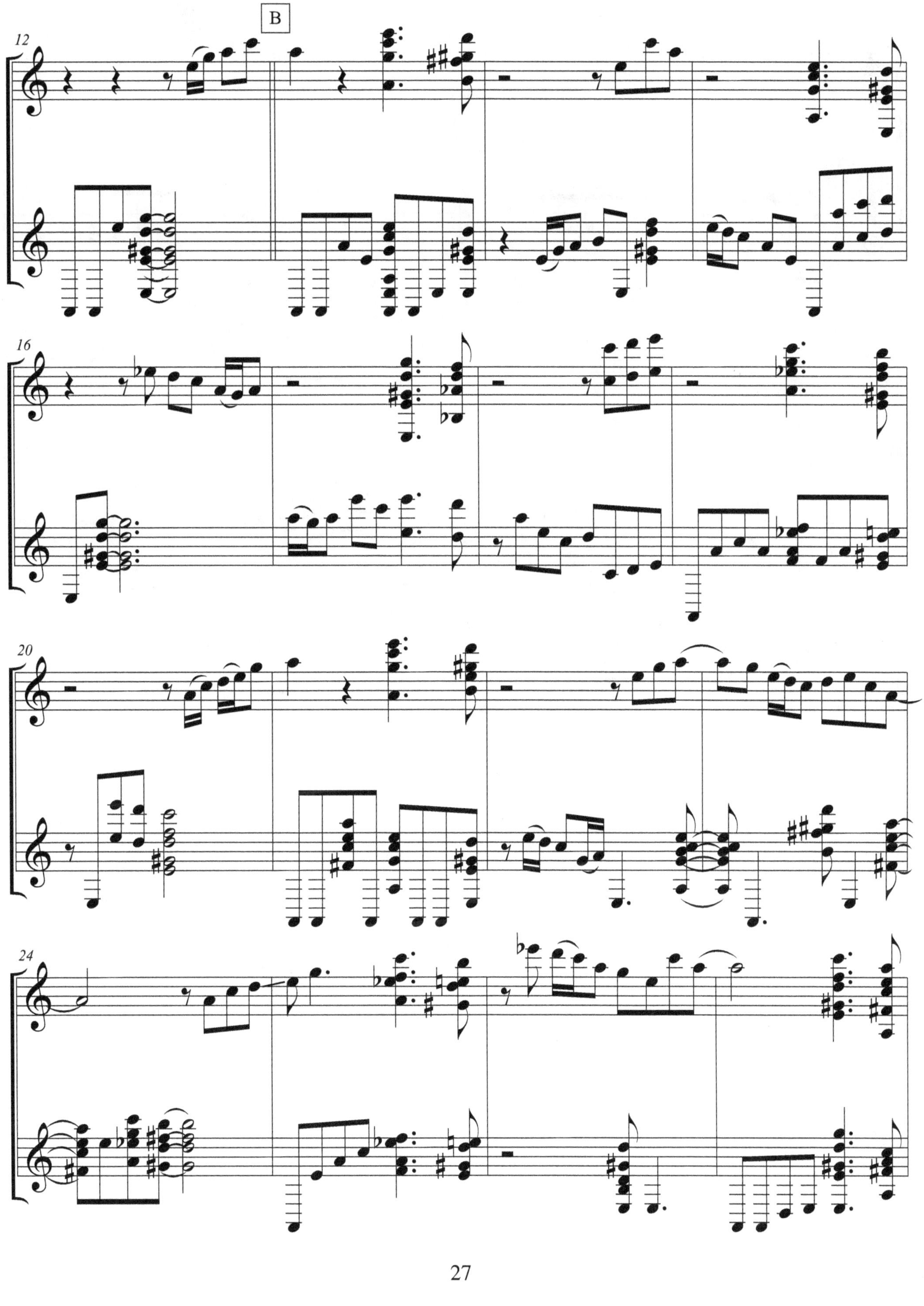
12
B
16
20
24

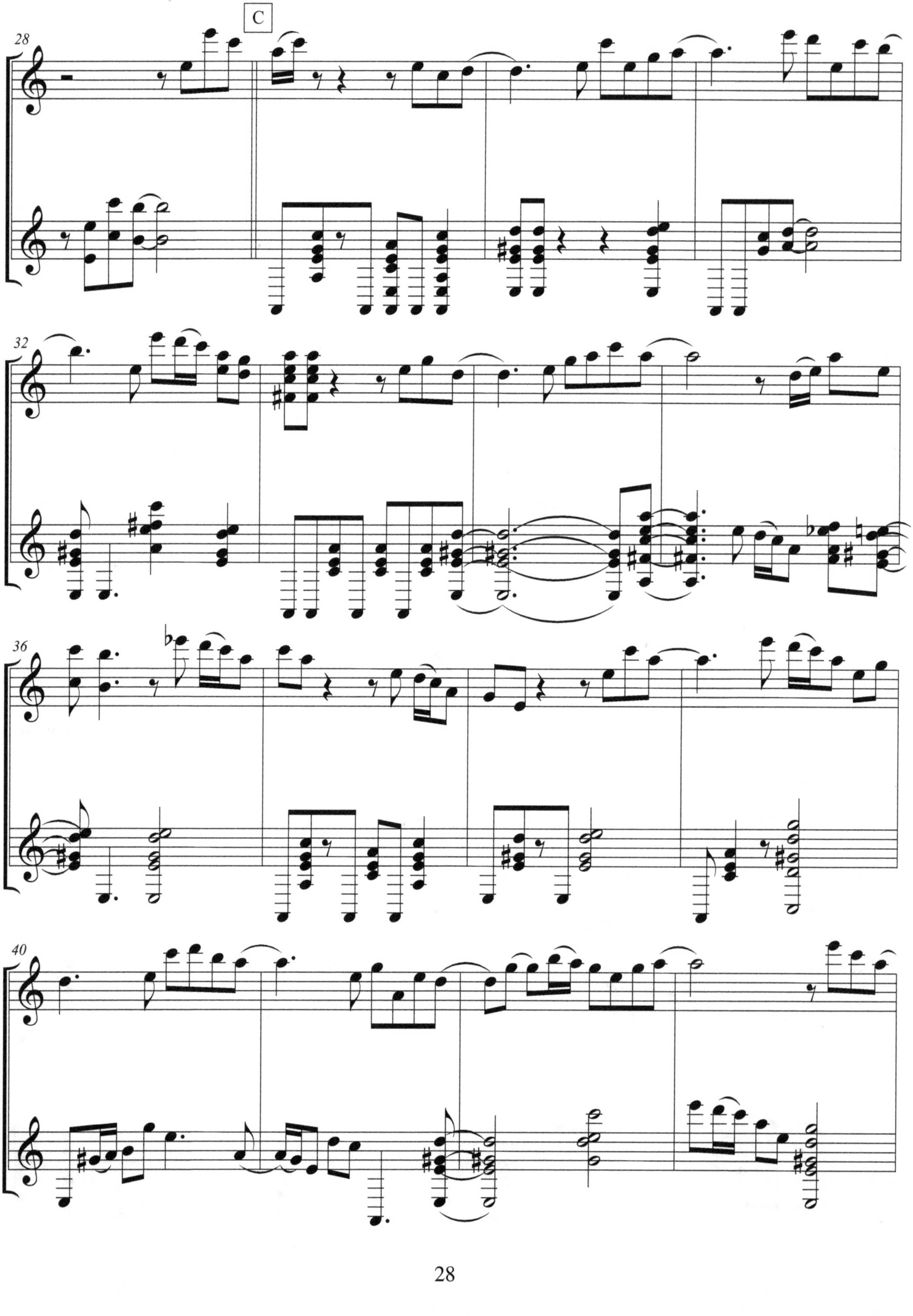
28
C
32
36
40

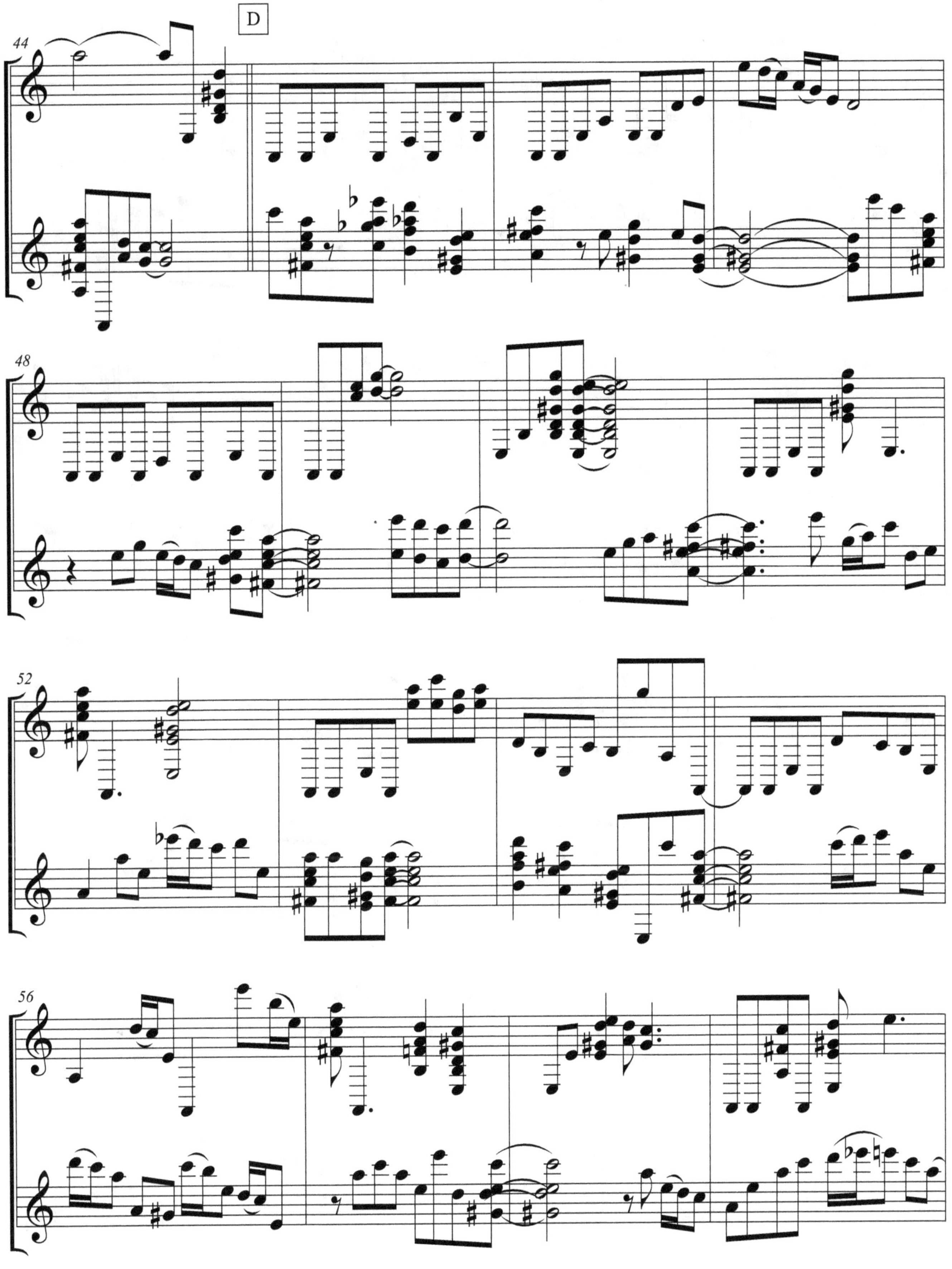
44
D
48
52
56

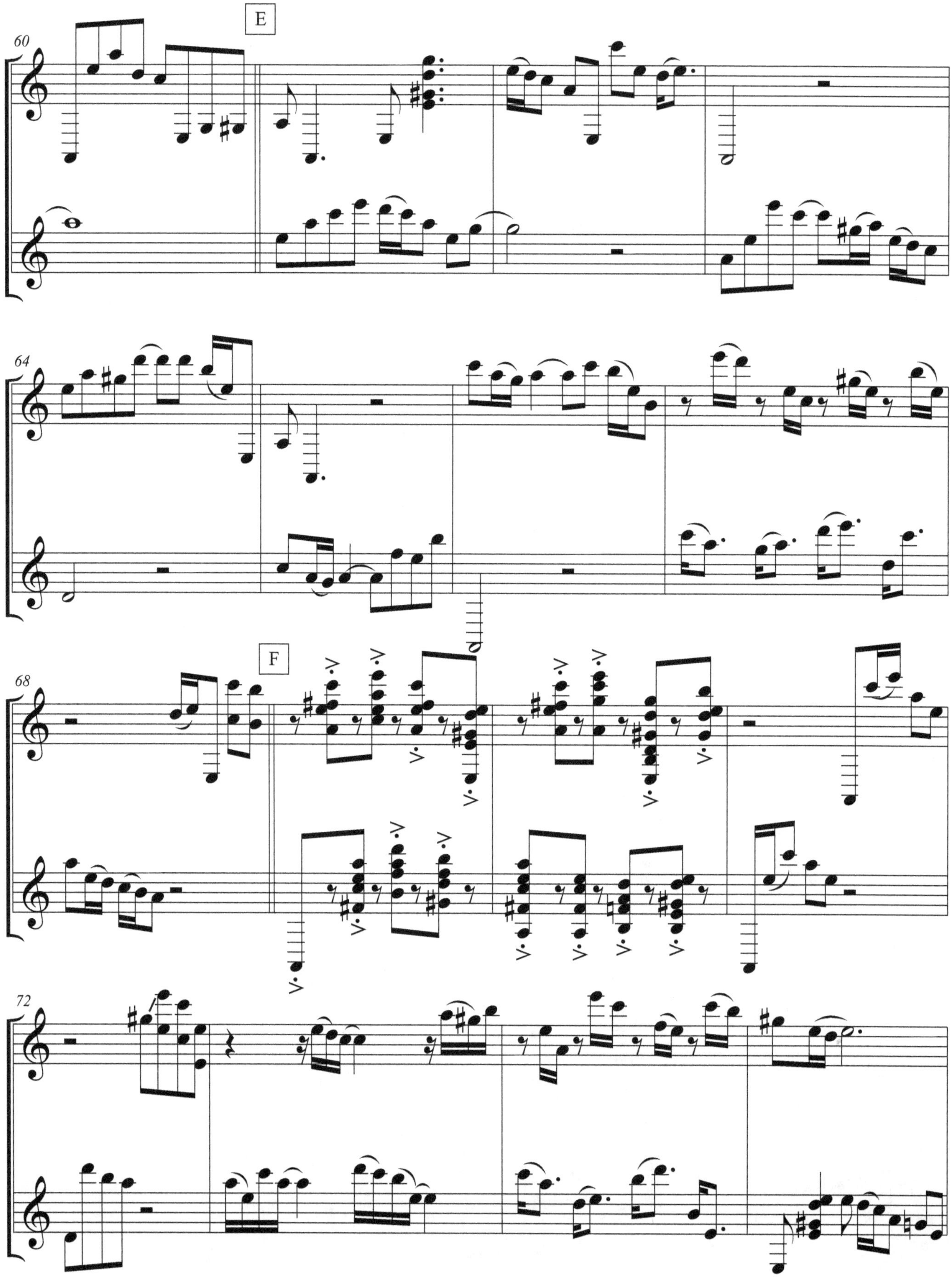
60
E
64
68
F
72

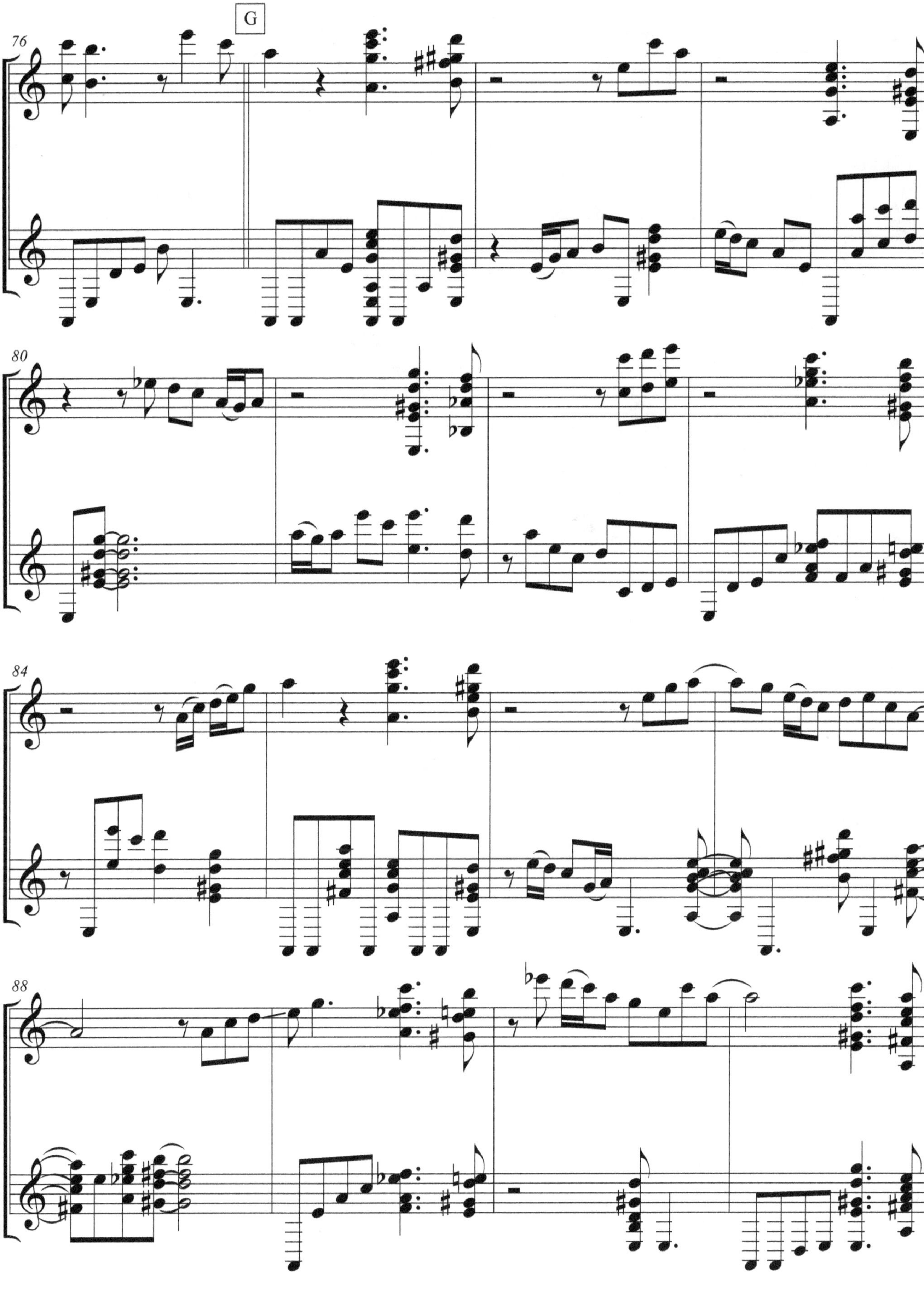
76
G
80
84
88

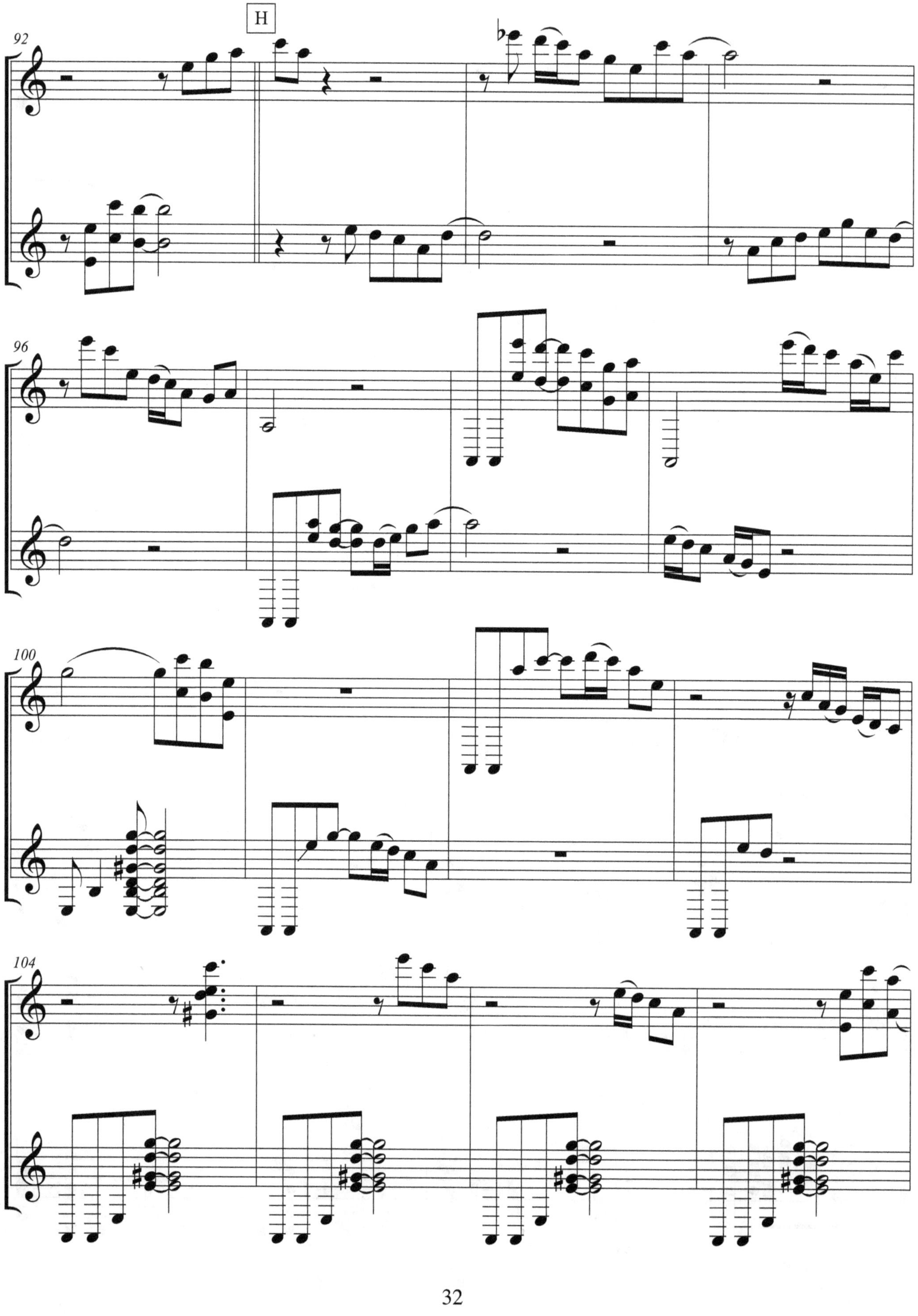
92
H
96
100
104

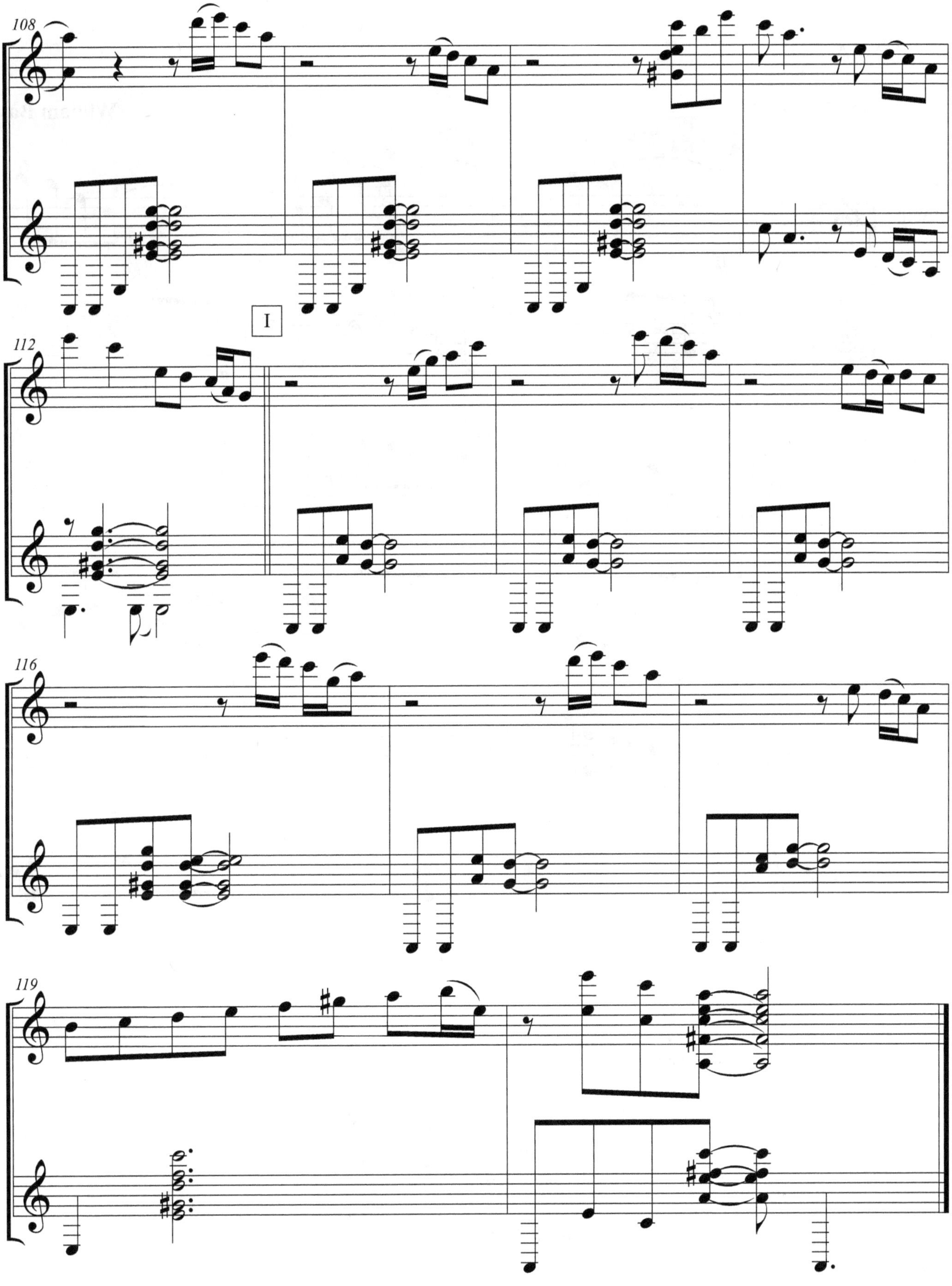
108
I
112
116
119

Elegy for Two Guitars

⑦ = A

Adante ♩ = 82

William Bay

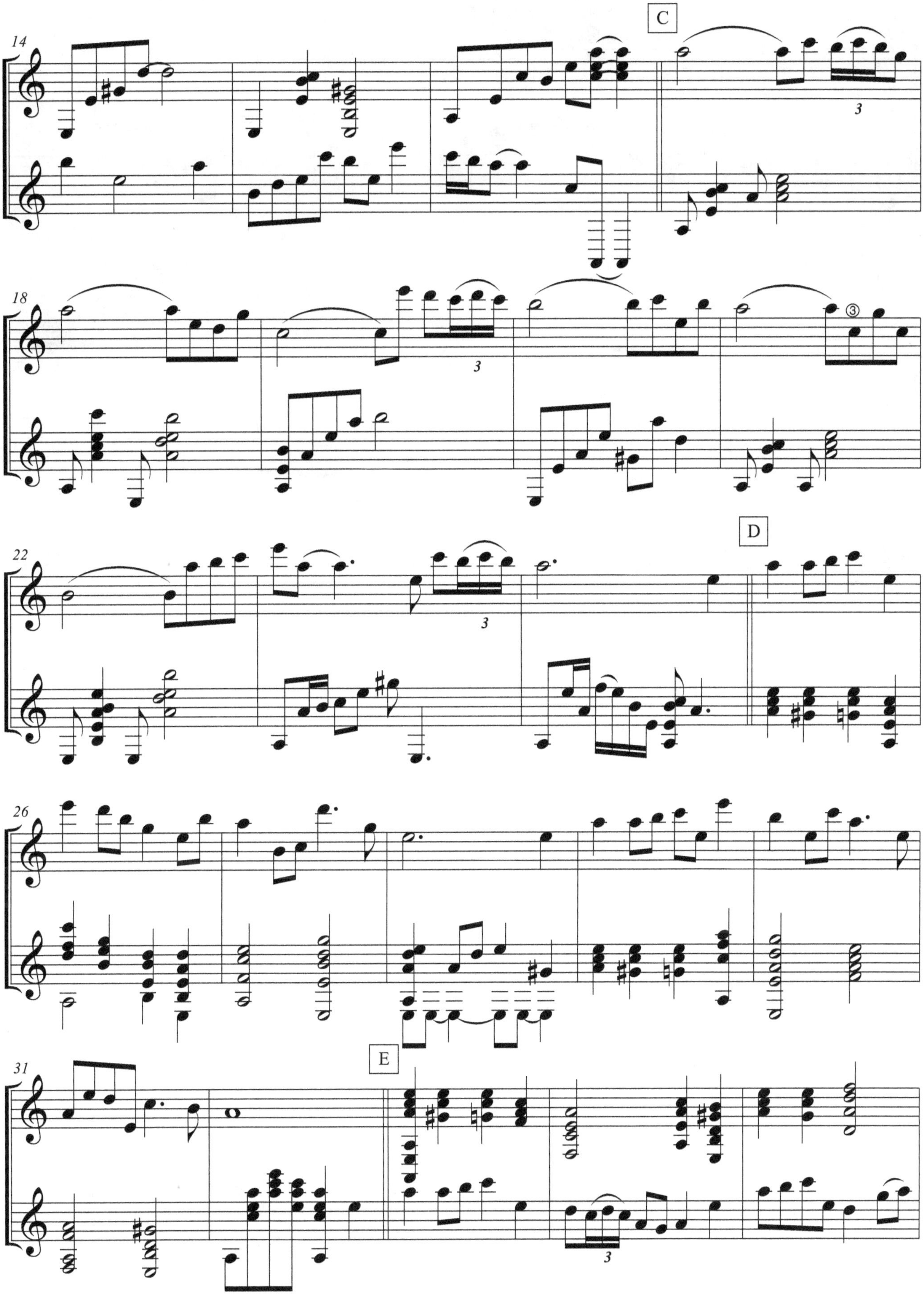
C
D
E
14
18
22
26
31

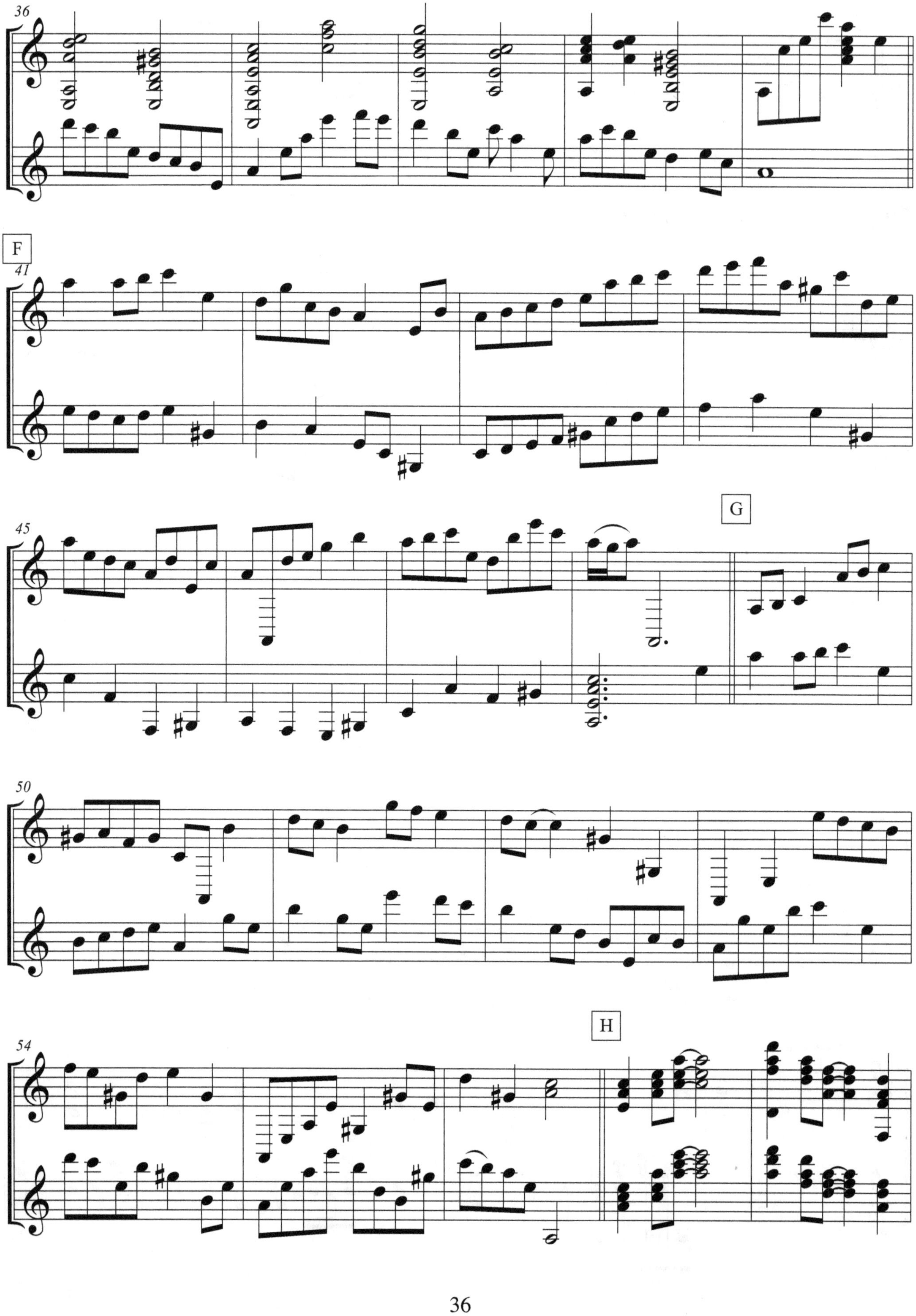
36
F
41
45
G
50
54
H

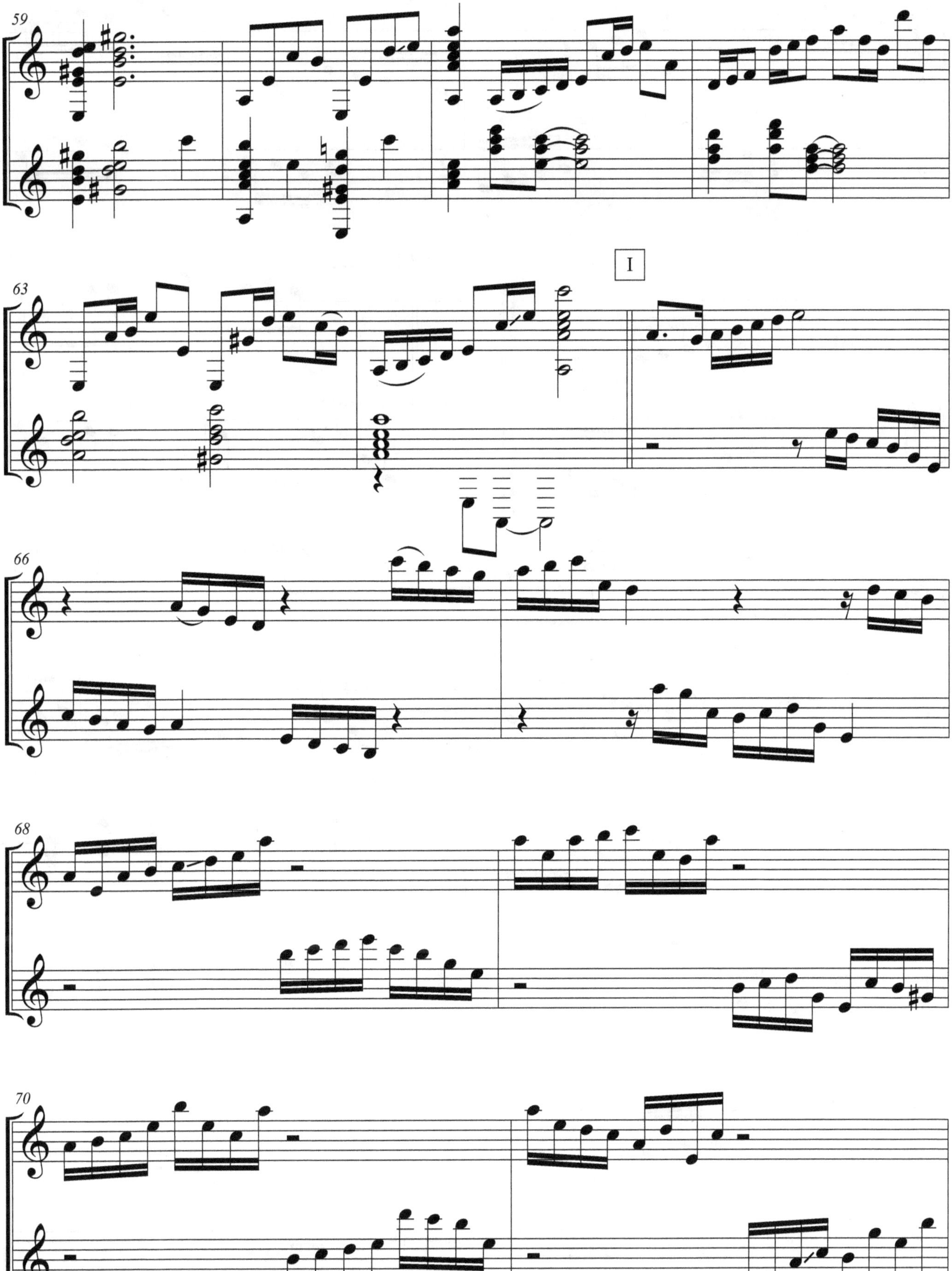
59
63
I
66
68
70

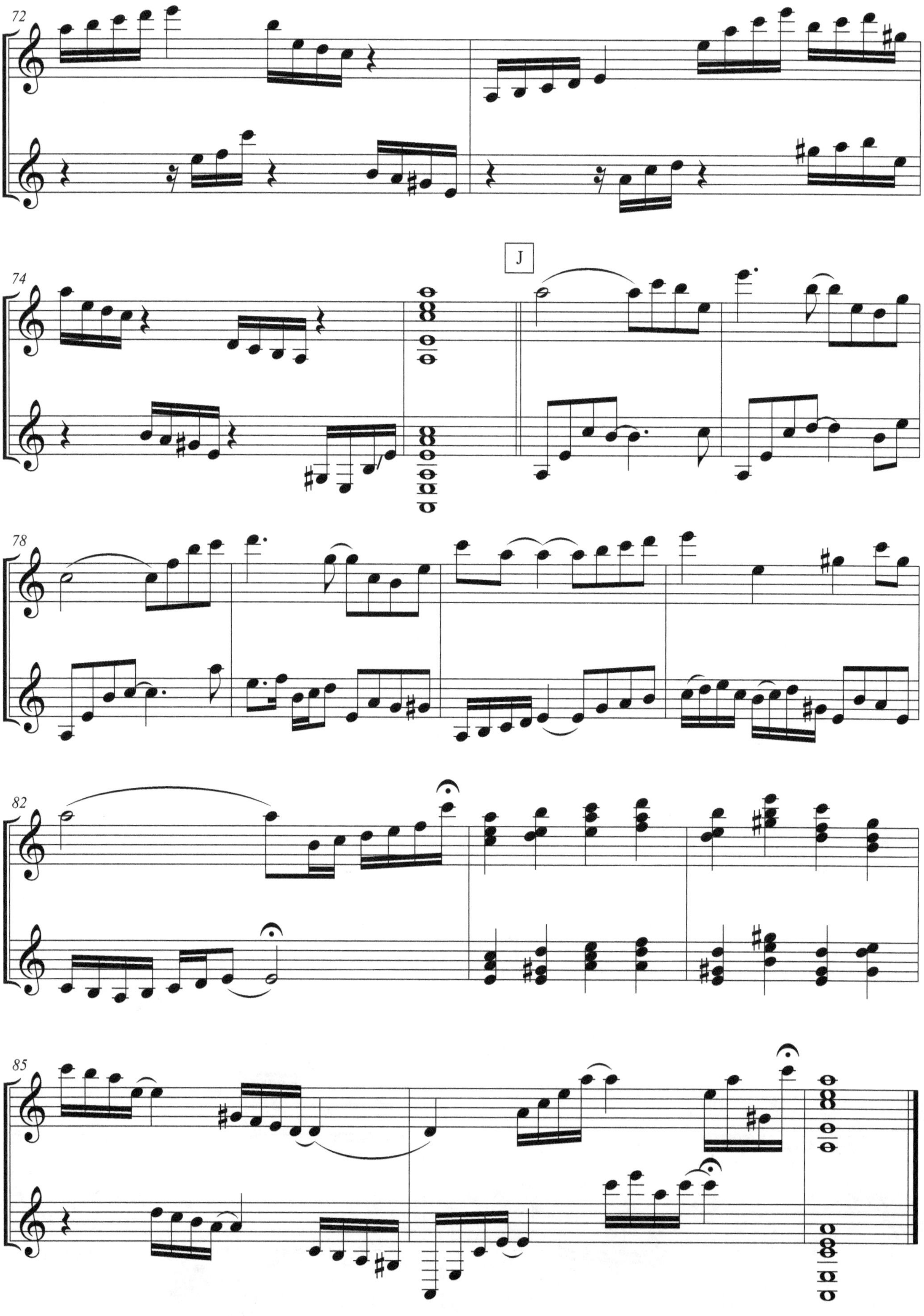
72
74
J
78
82
85

This page has been left blank
to avoid awkward page turns.

Star in the Night

⑦ = A

Dropped D Tuning

William Bay

Adagio ♩. = 80

2

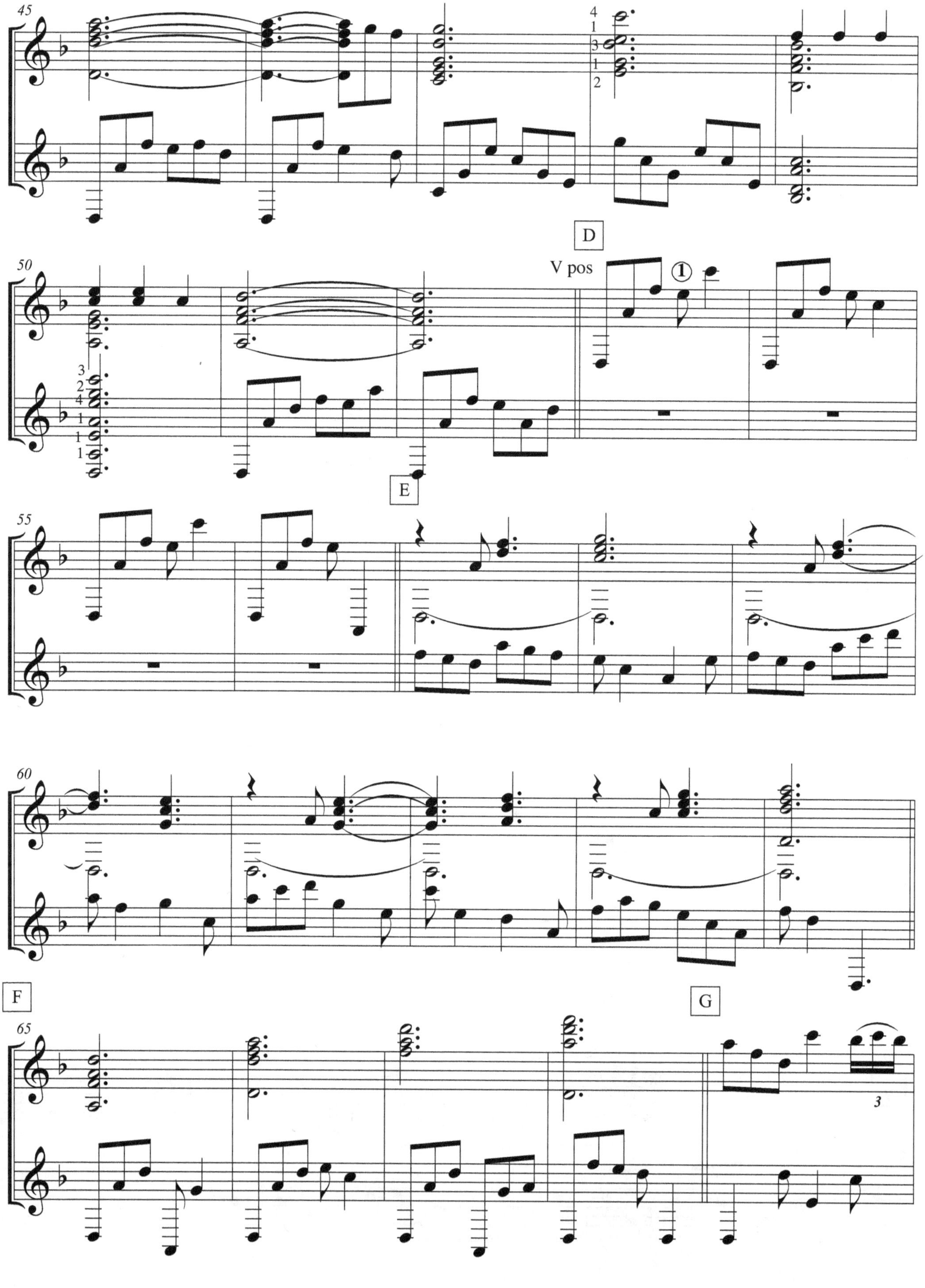
D
V pos
E
F
G

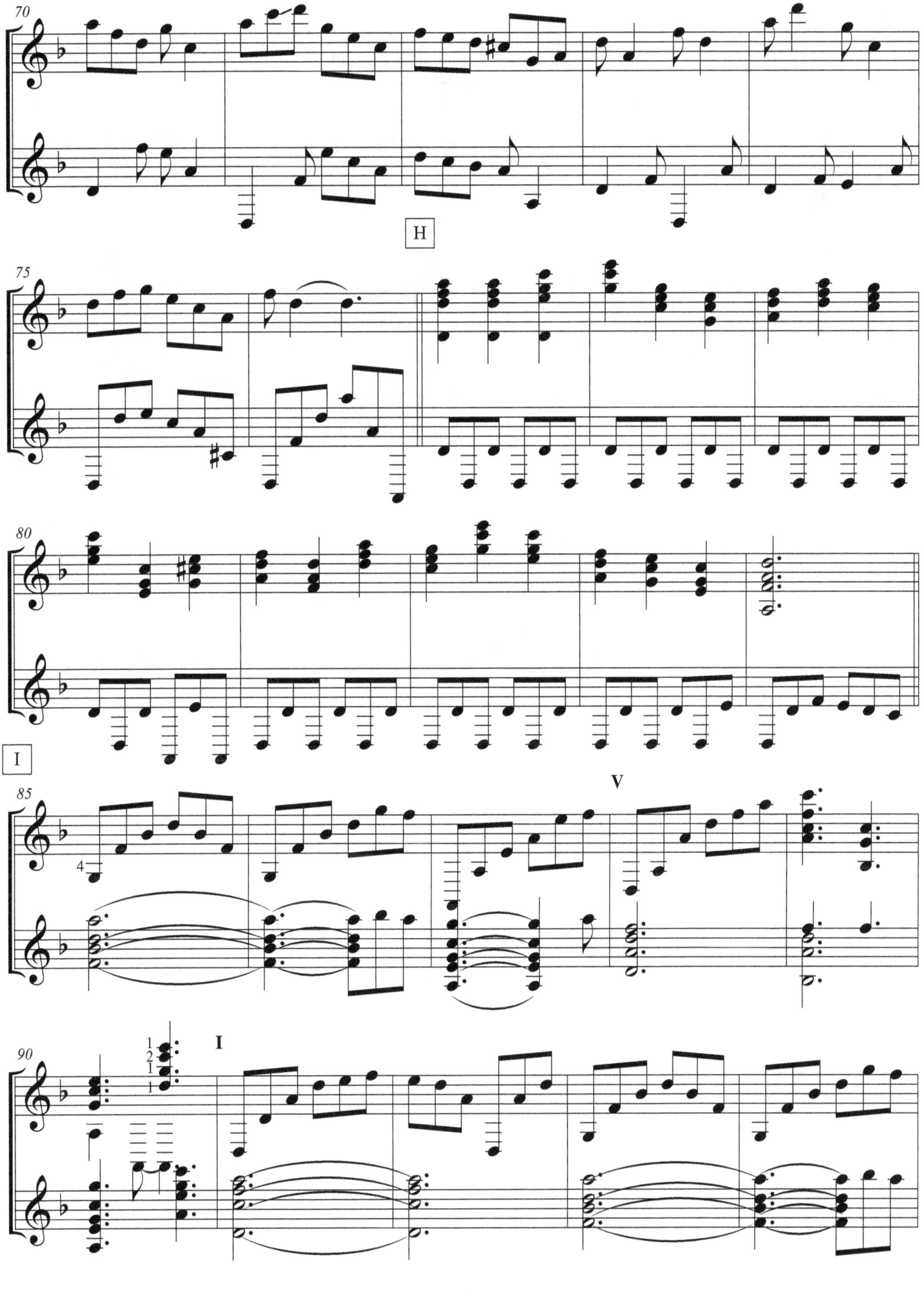
70
H
75
80
I
85
4
V
90
1
2
1
1
I

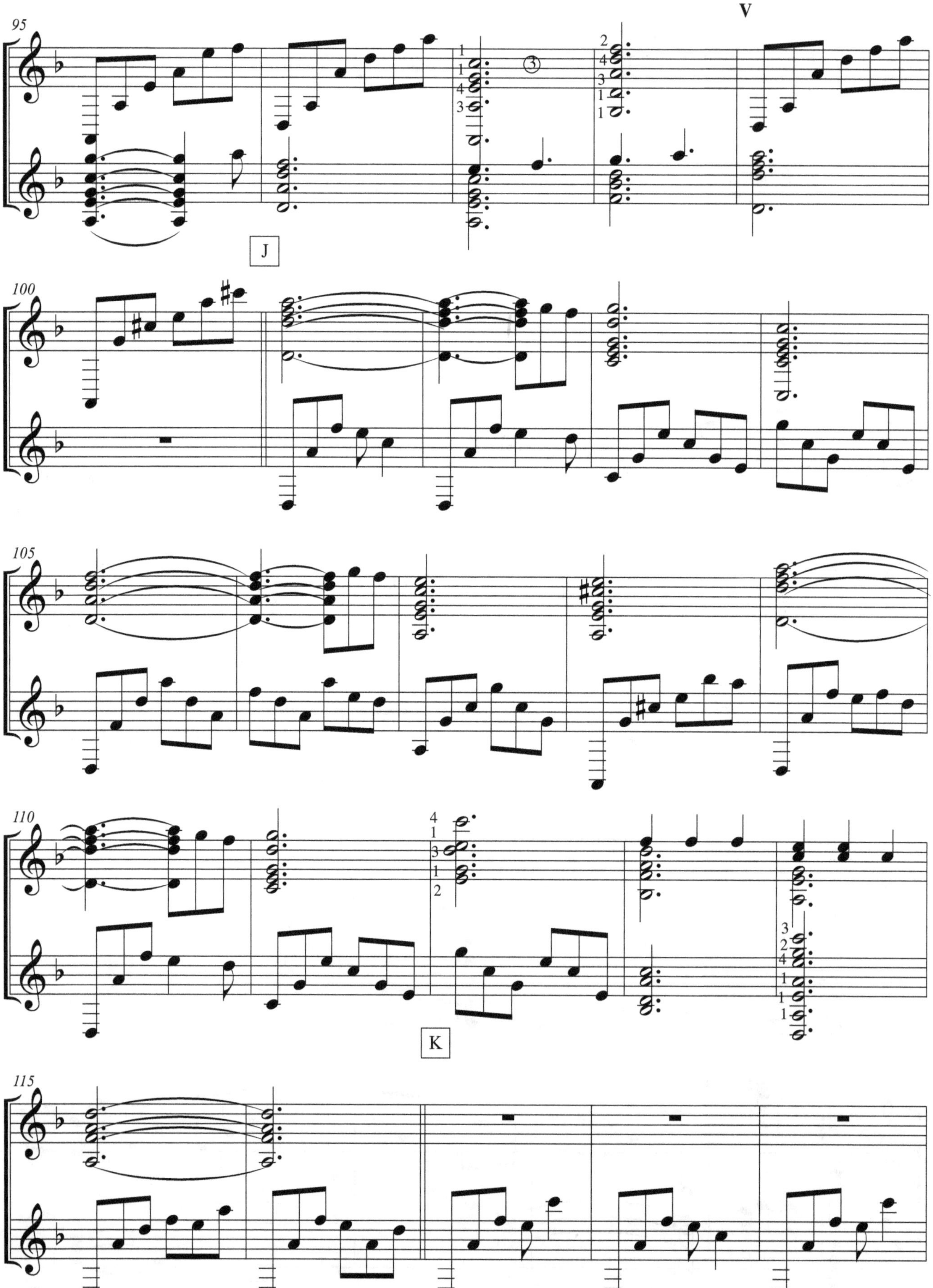
95
V
J
100
105
110
K
115

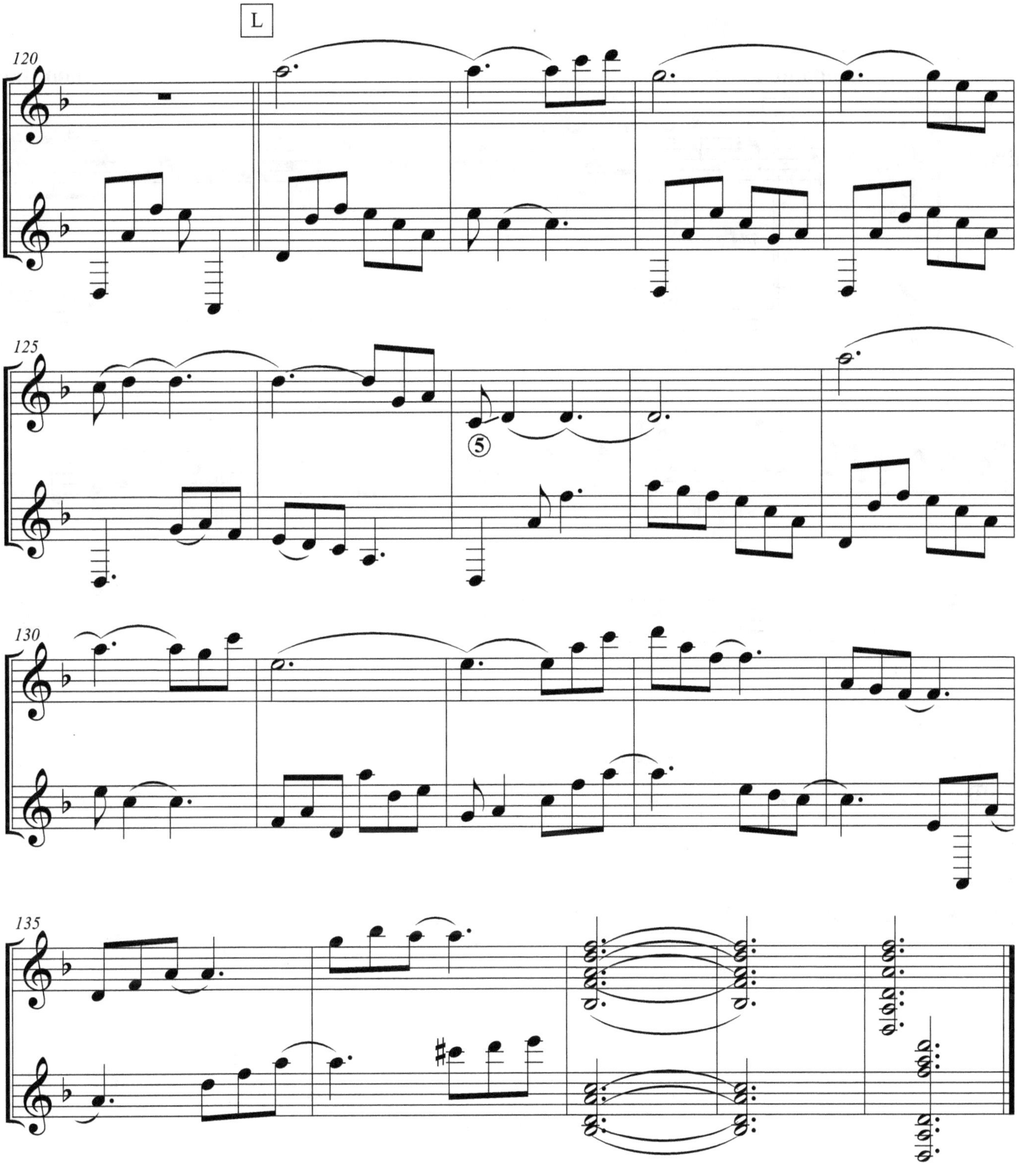
L
120
125
5
130
135

Canticle

Andante ♩ = 78

William Bay

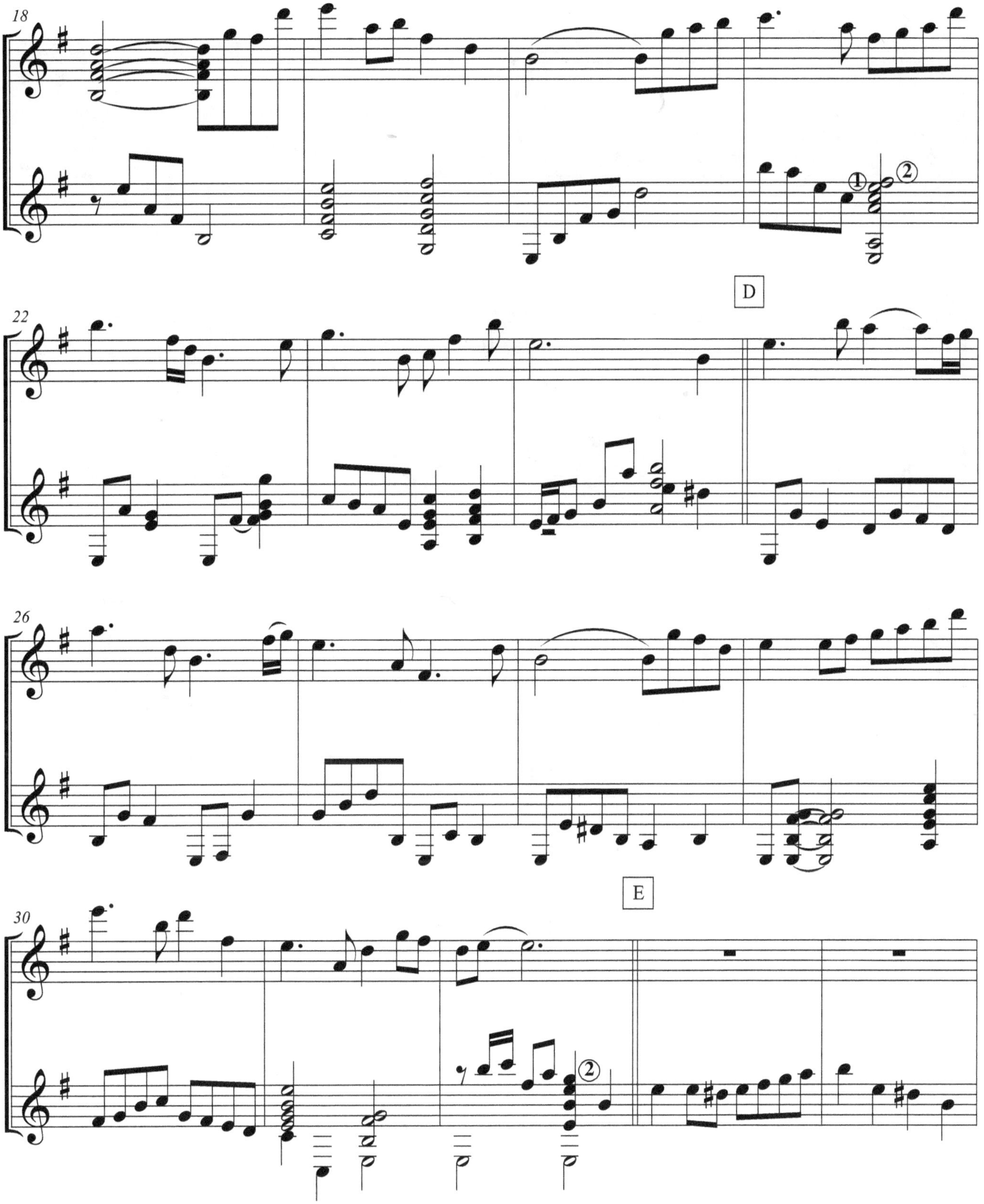
18
①
②
22
D
26
30
E
②

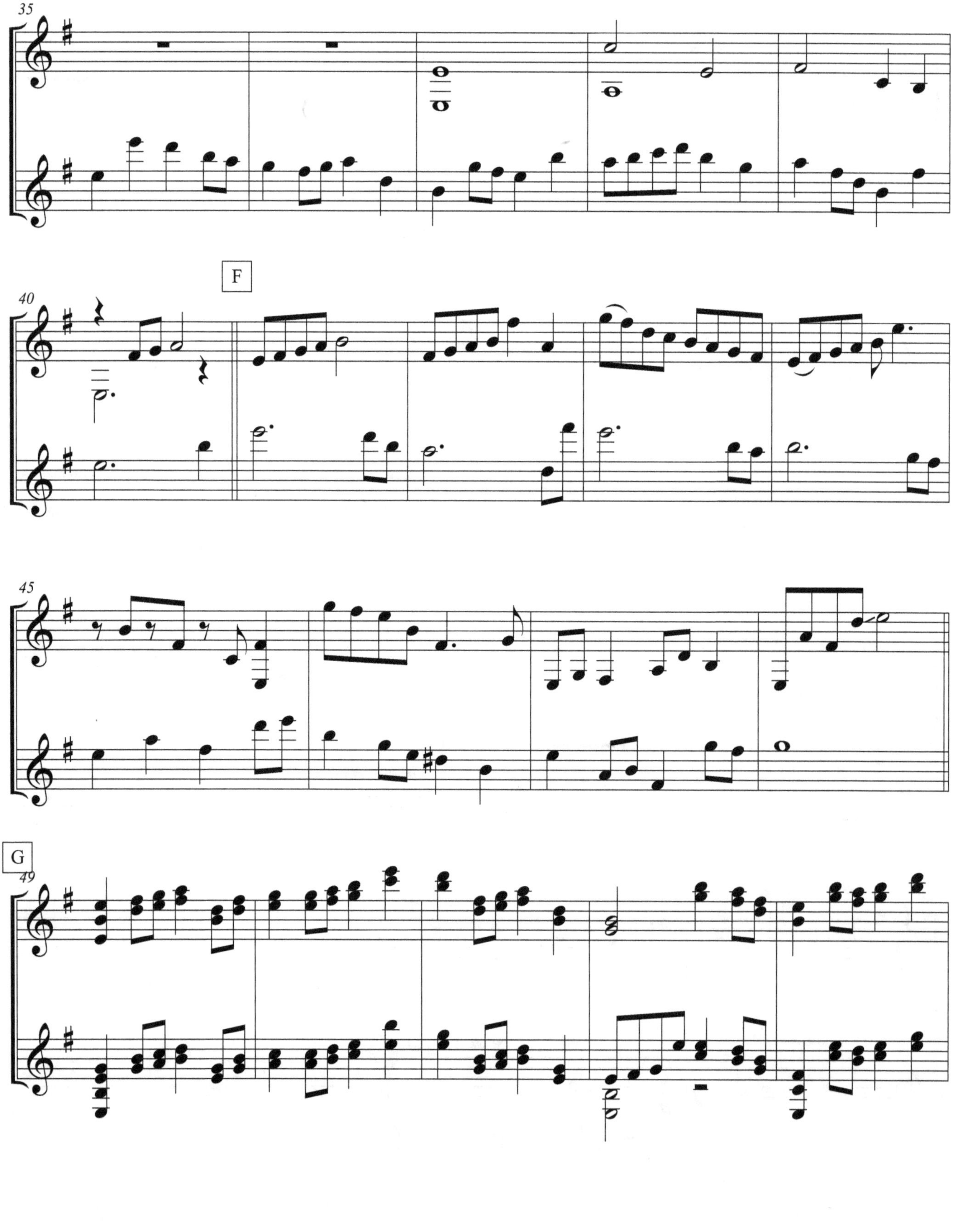
35
40
F
45
G
49

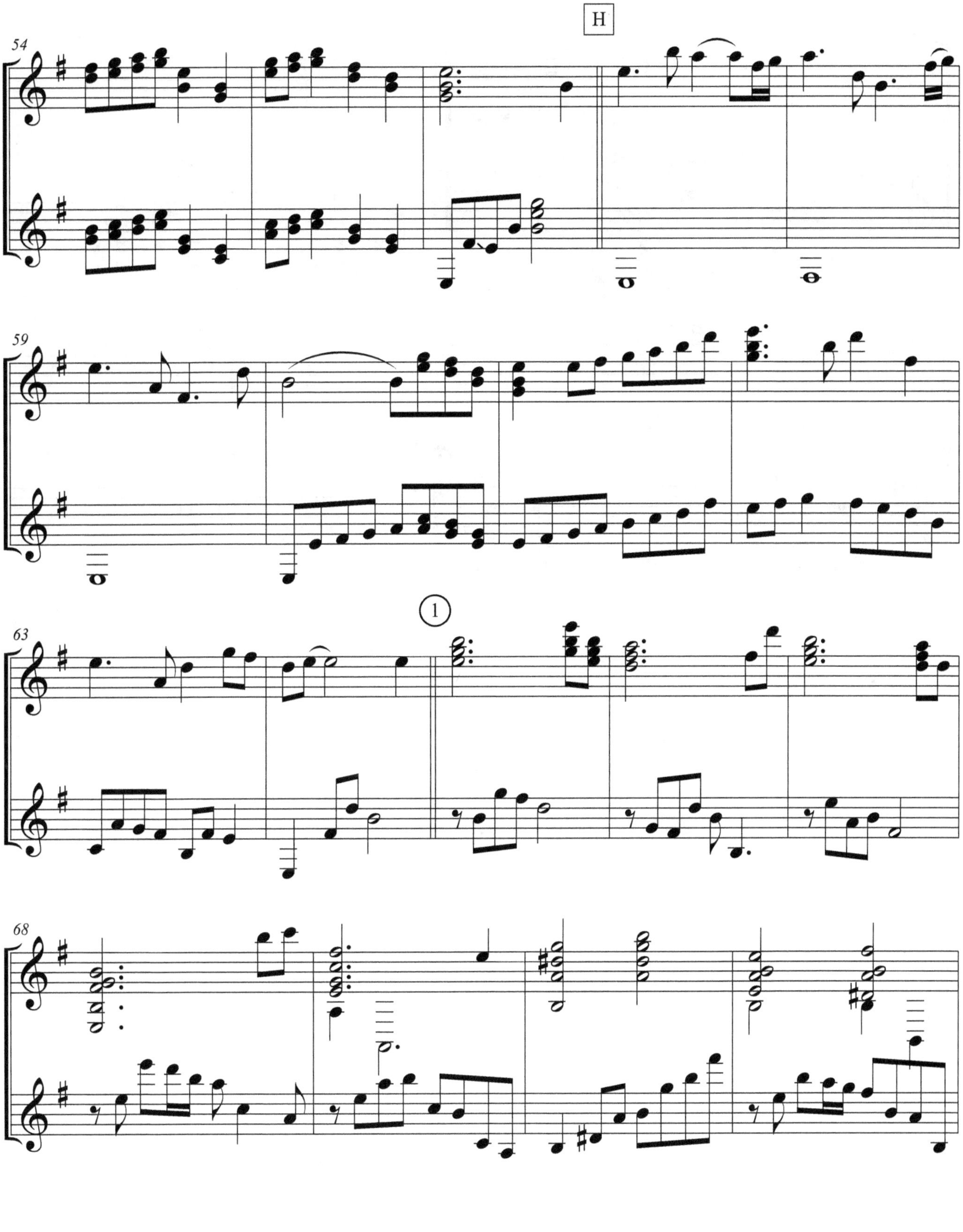
H
54
59
1
63
68

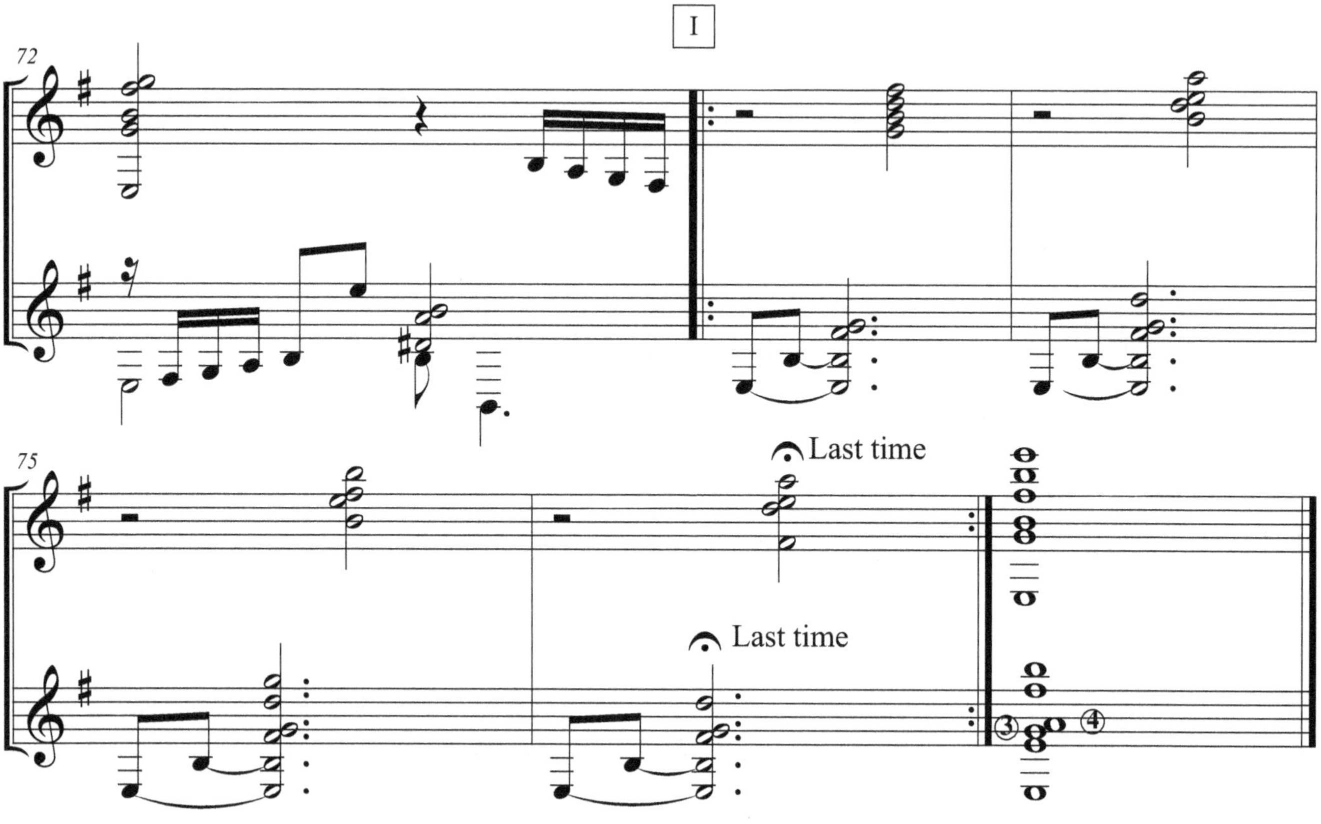
I
72
75
Last time
Last time
③
④

This page has been left blank
to avoid awkward page turns.

Waves

William Bay

52

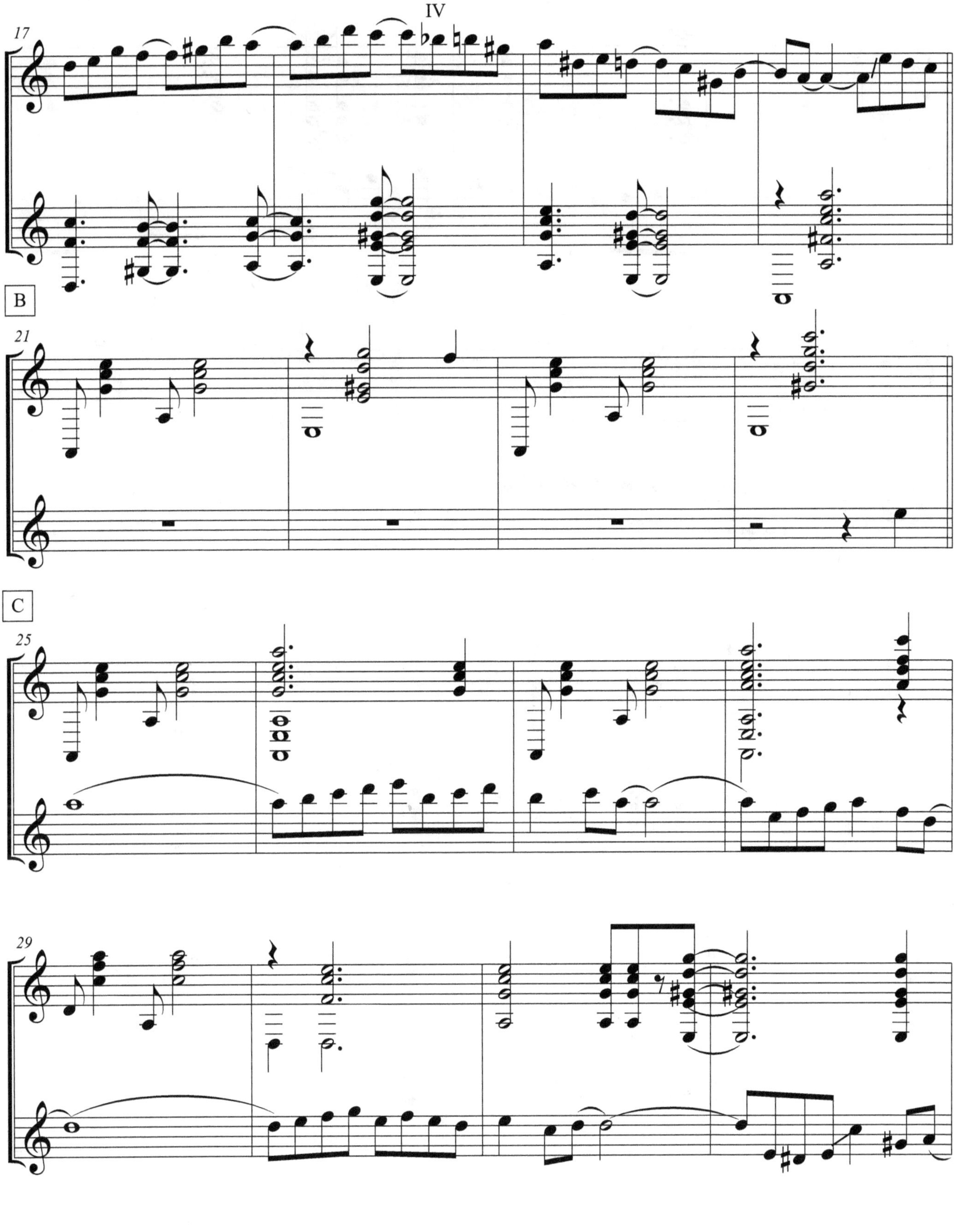
17
IV
B
21
C
25
29

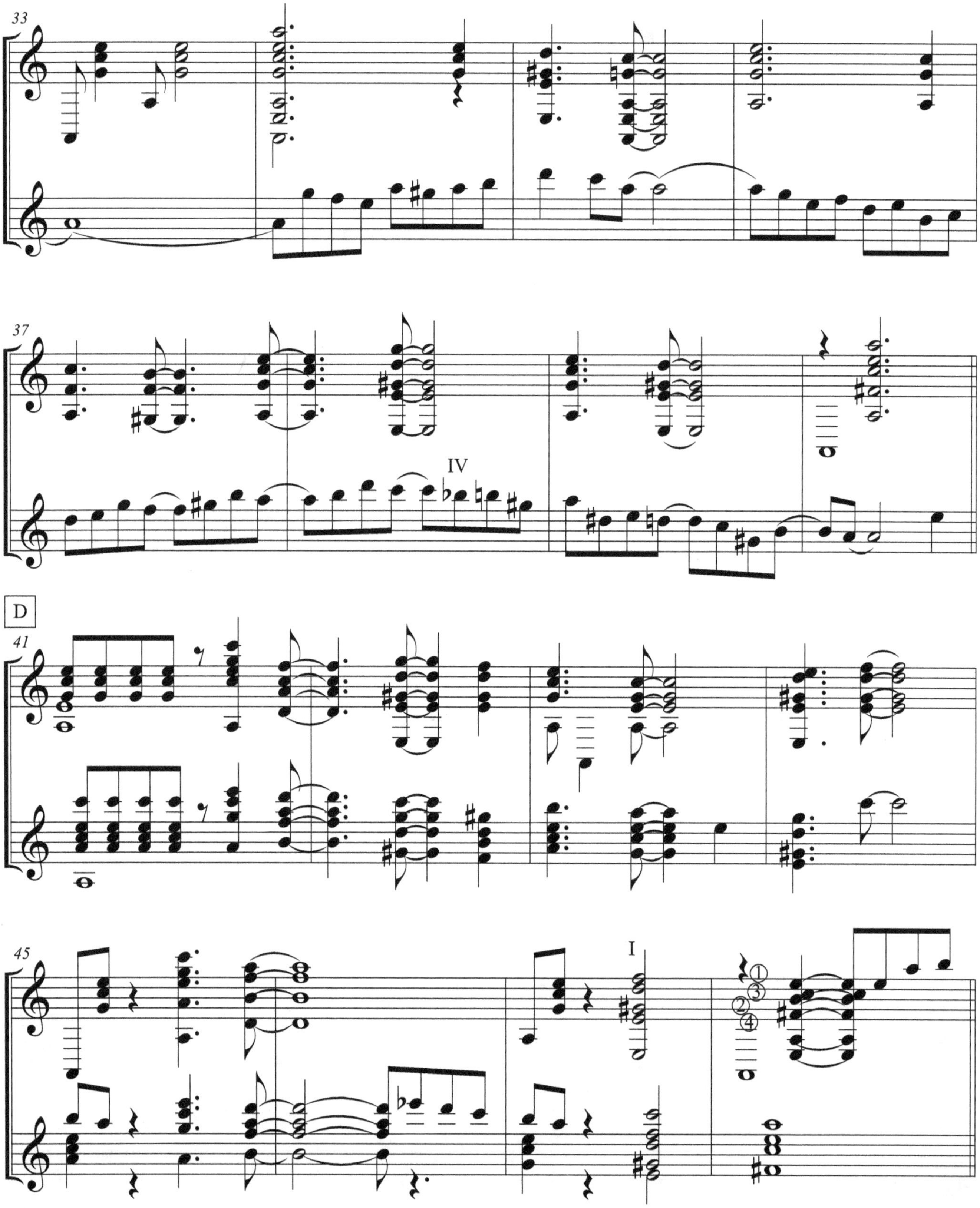
33
37
IV
D
41
45
I

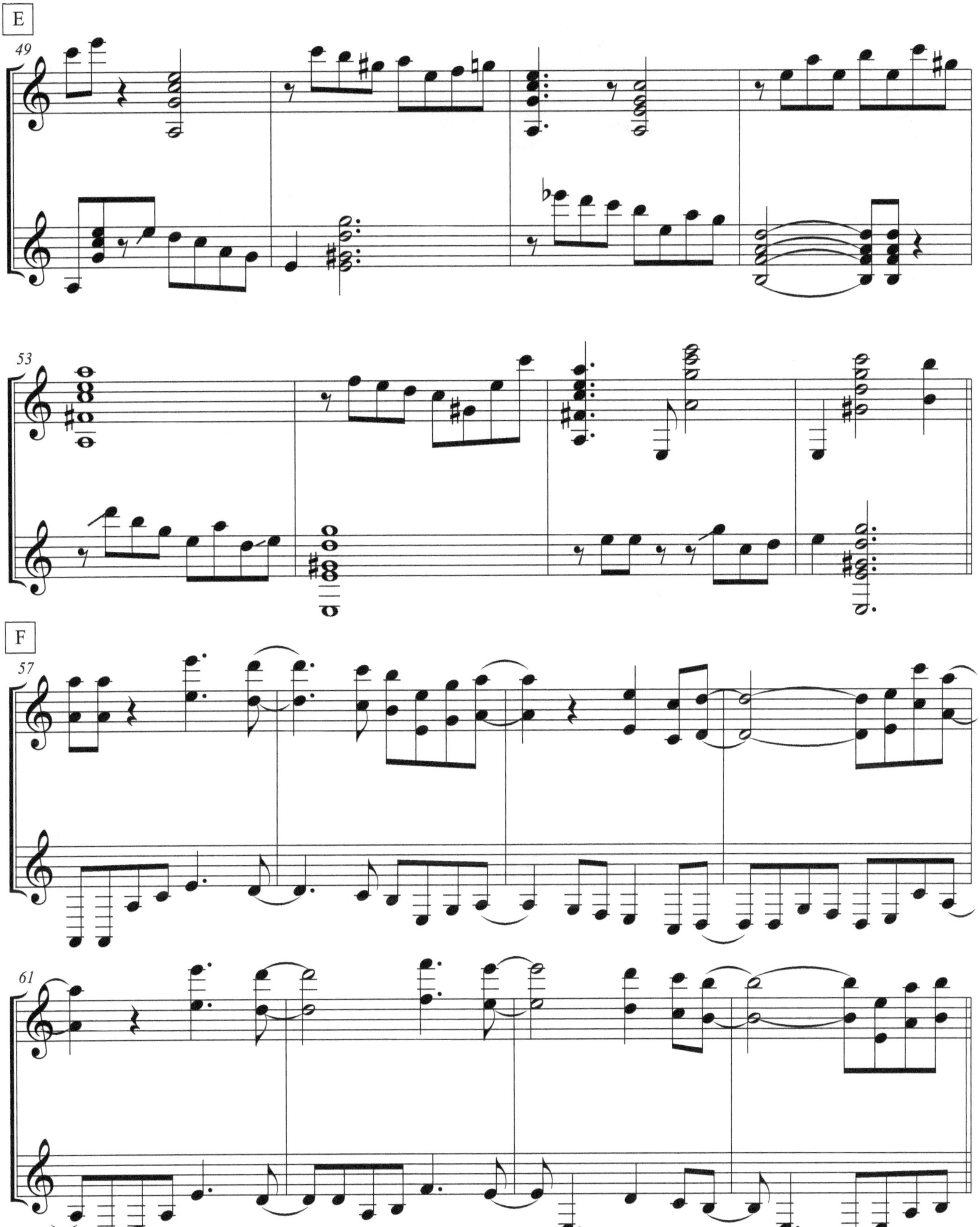
E
49
53
F
57
61

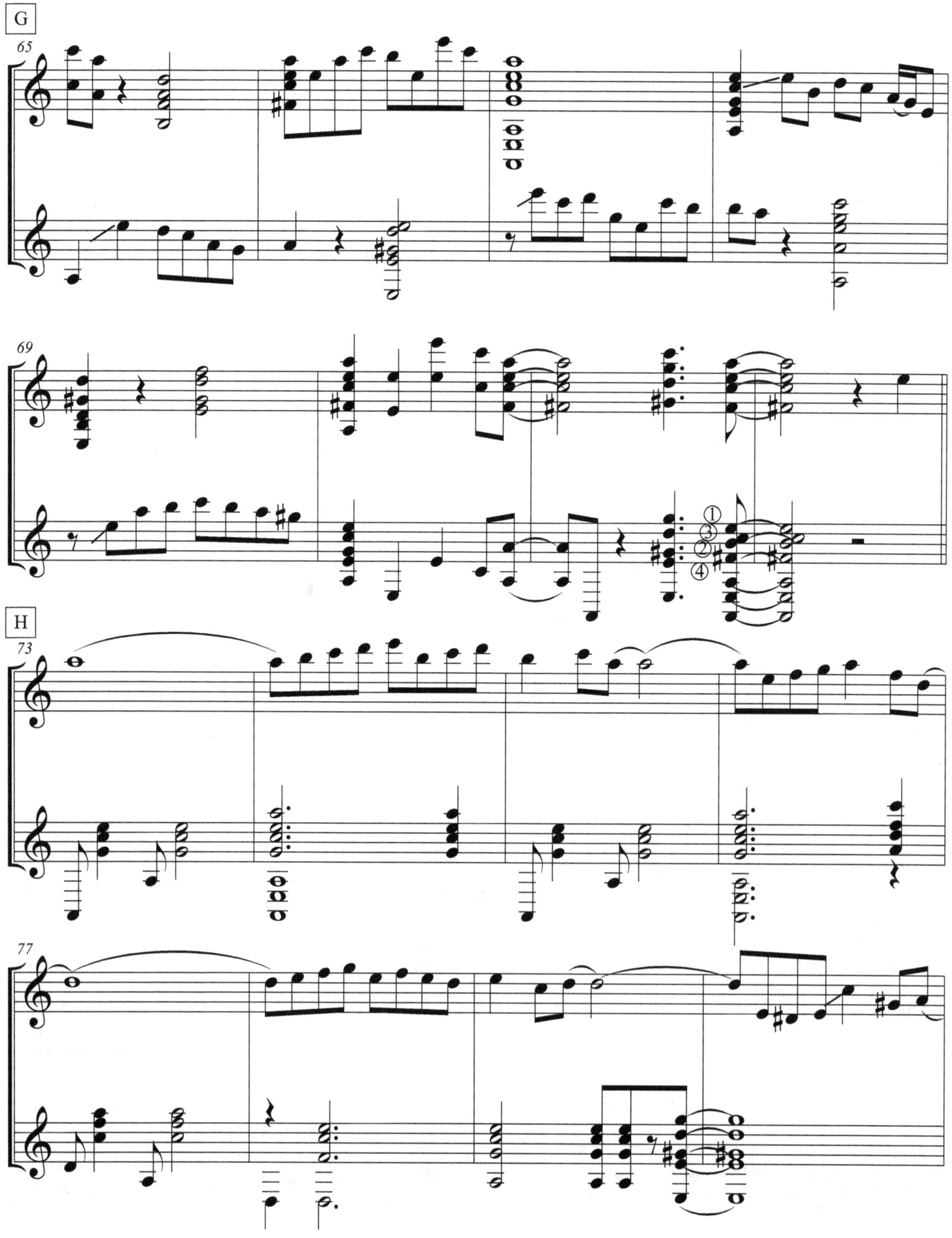
G
65
69
①
③
②
④
H
73
77

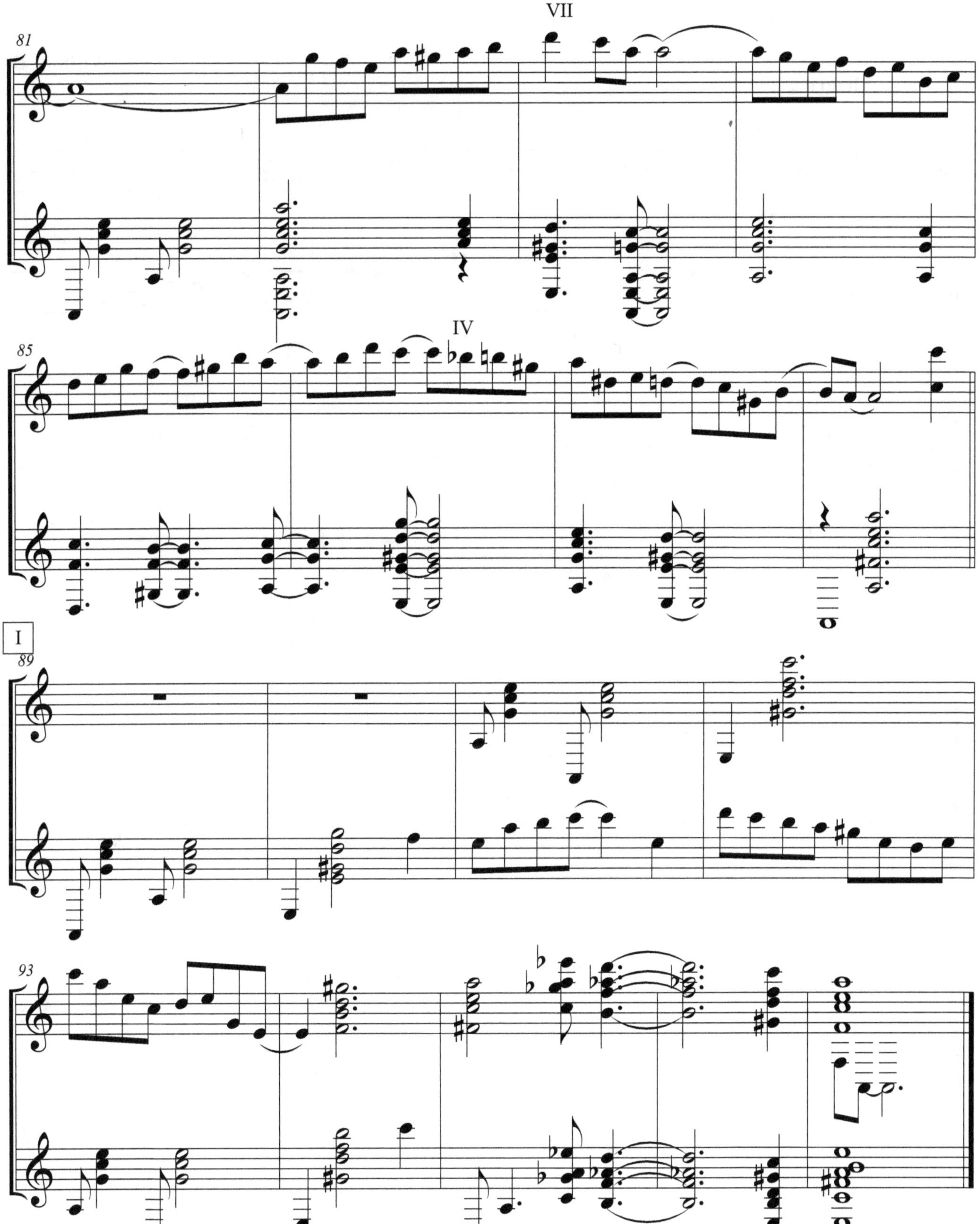
VII
81
85
IV
I
89
93

Beatitude

⑦ = A

Dropped D Tuning

William Bay

Allegro ♩ = 108

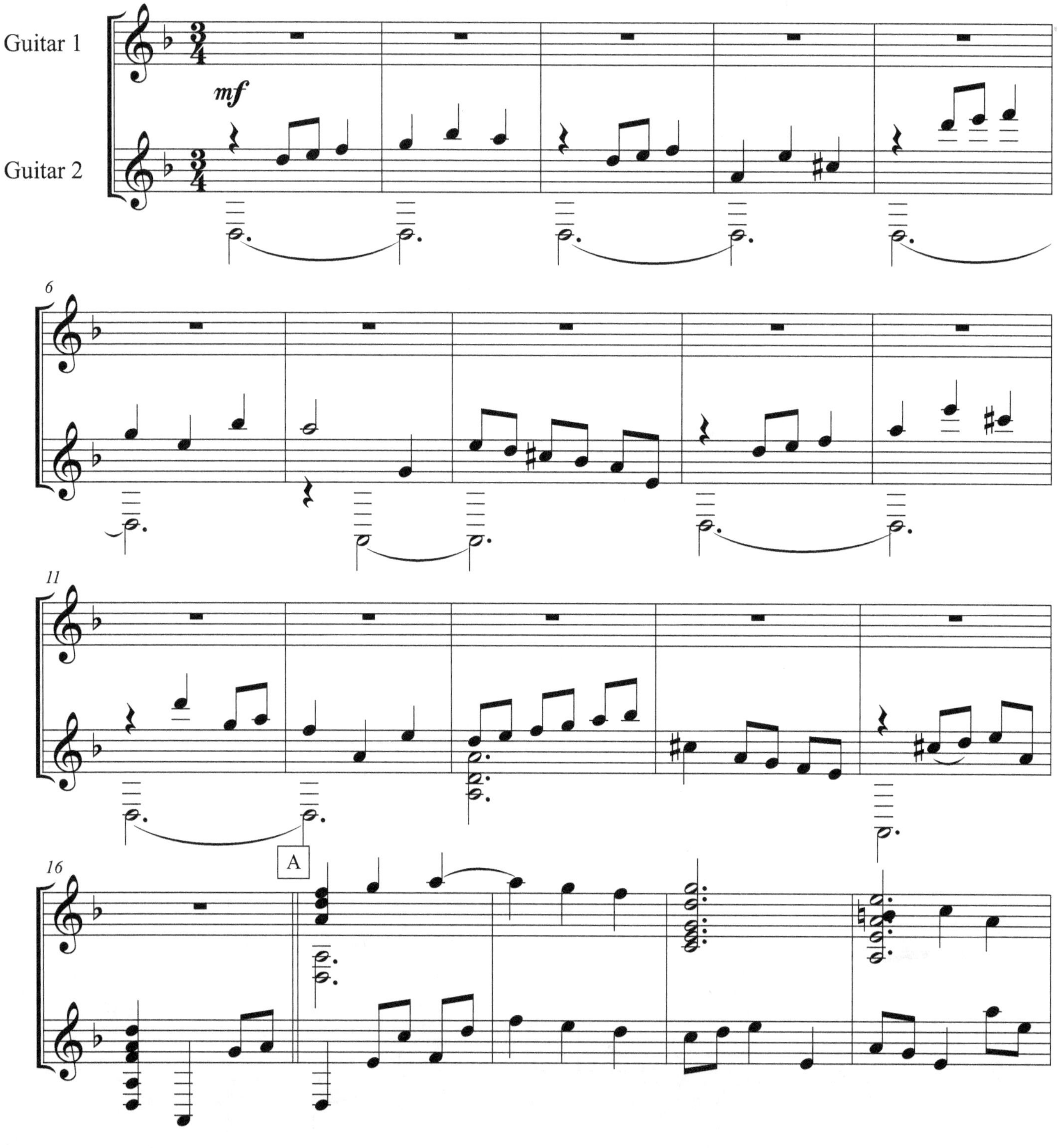

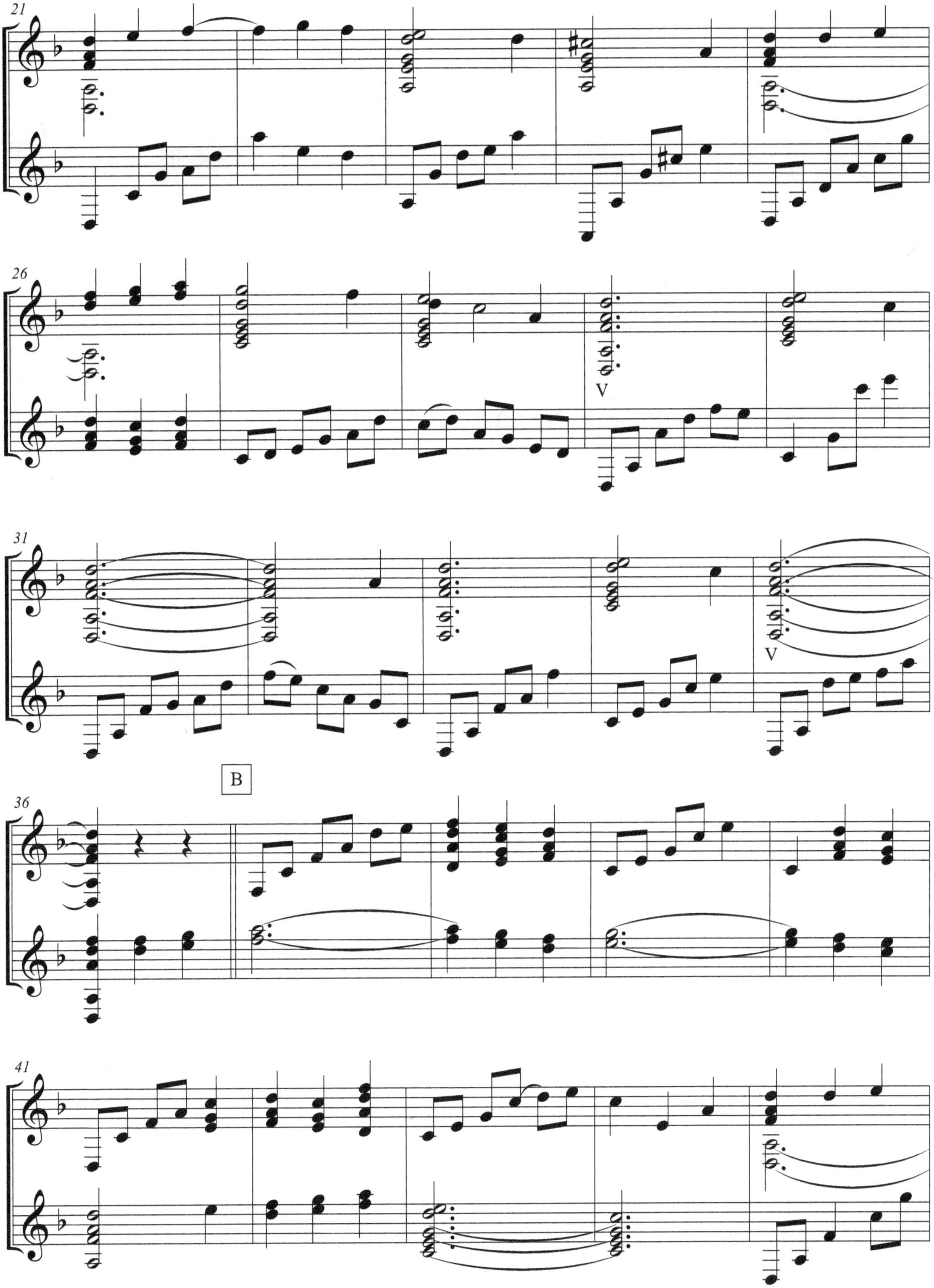
21
26
V
31
V
B
36
41

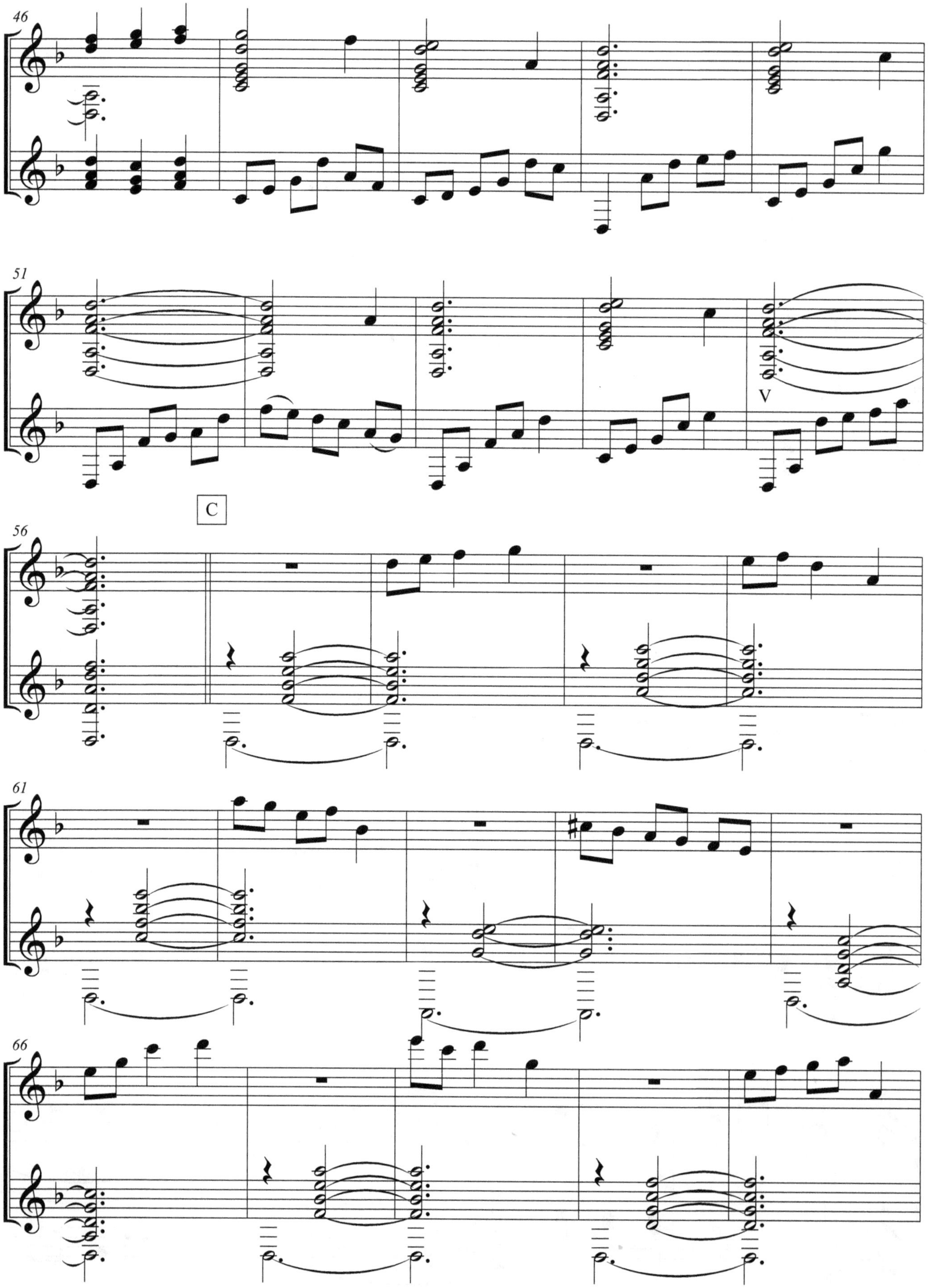
46
51
V
C
56
61
66

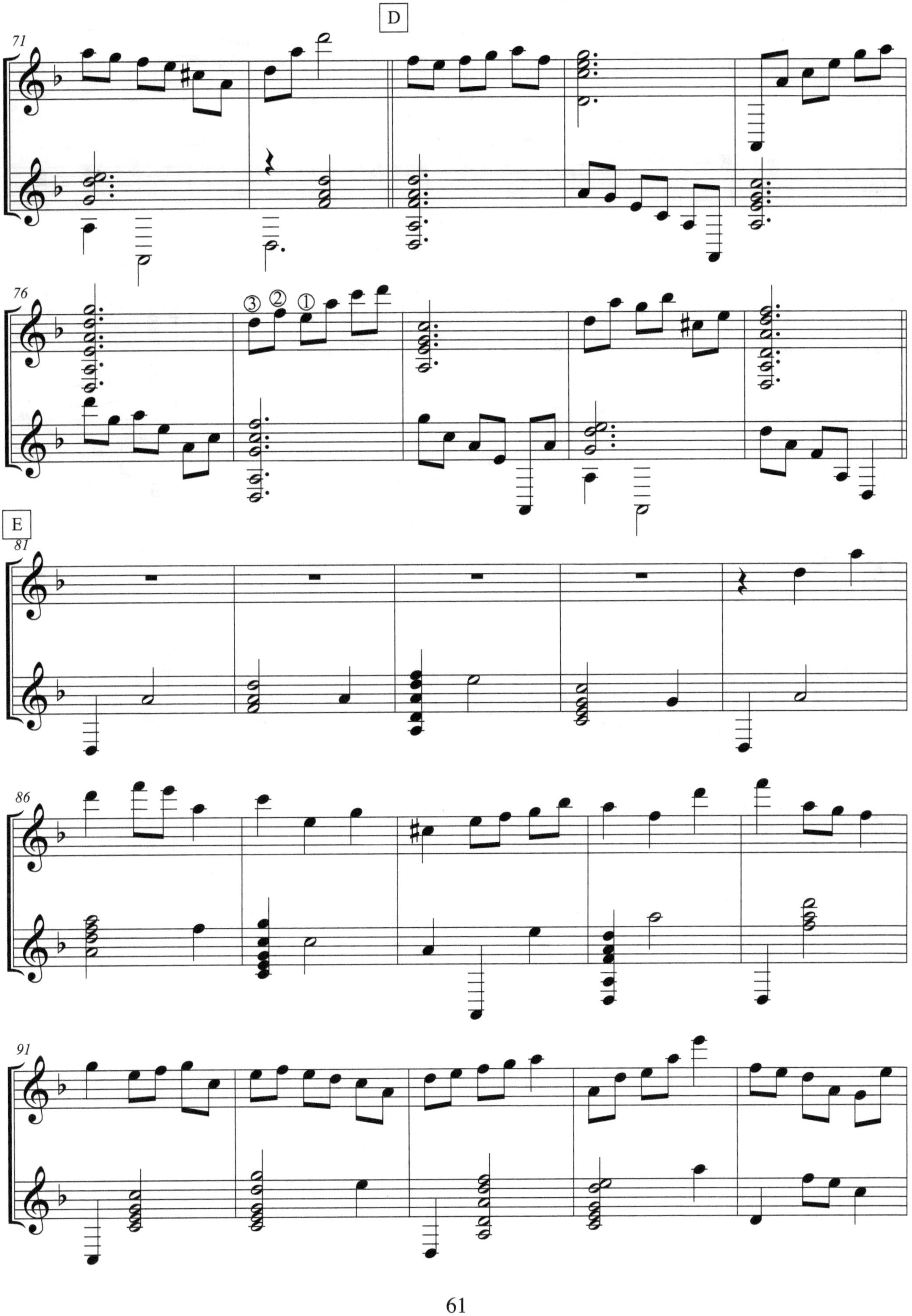
D
71
76
③ ② ①
E
81
86
91

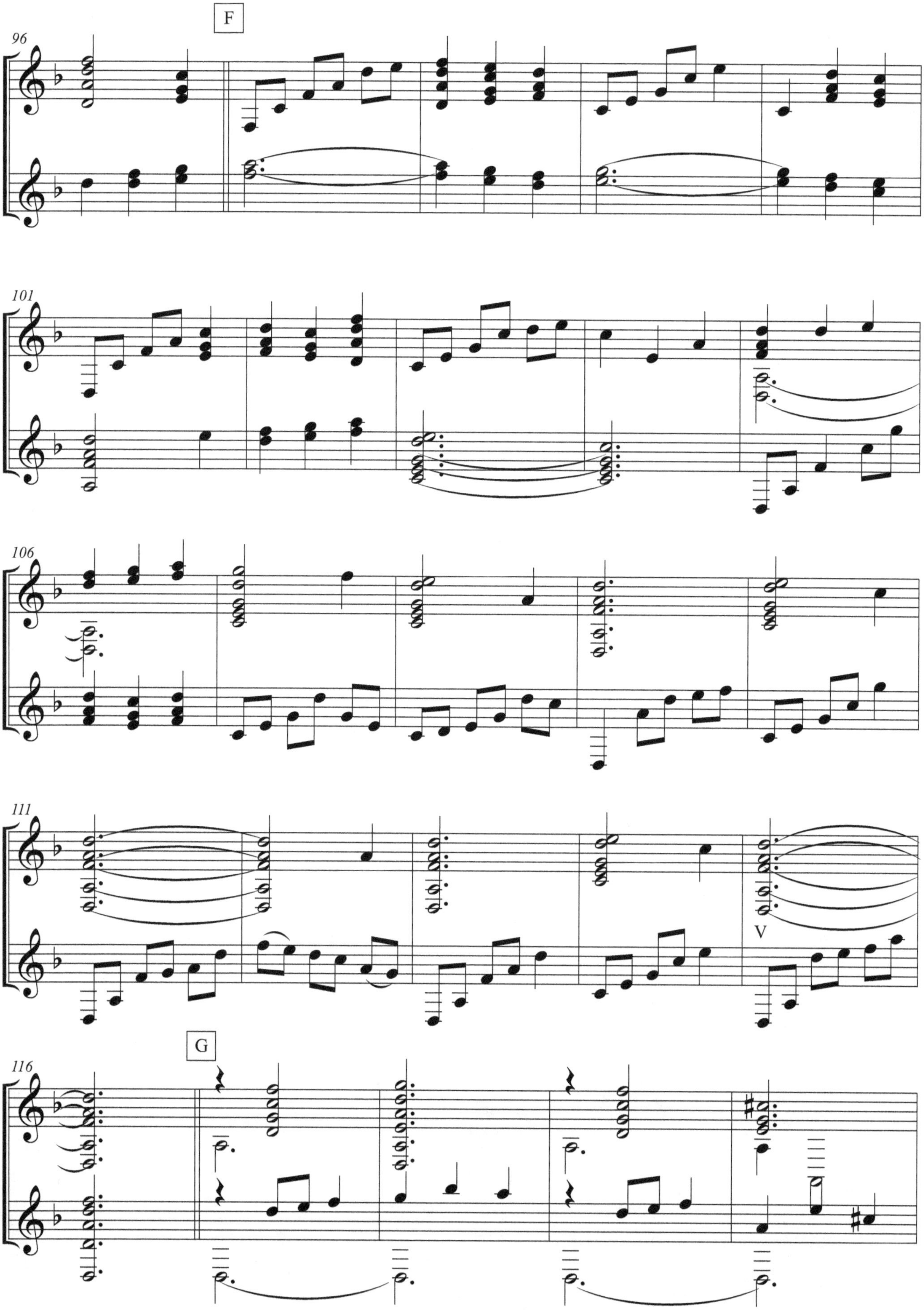
F
96
101
106
111
V
116
G

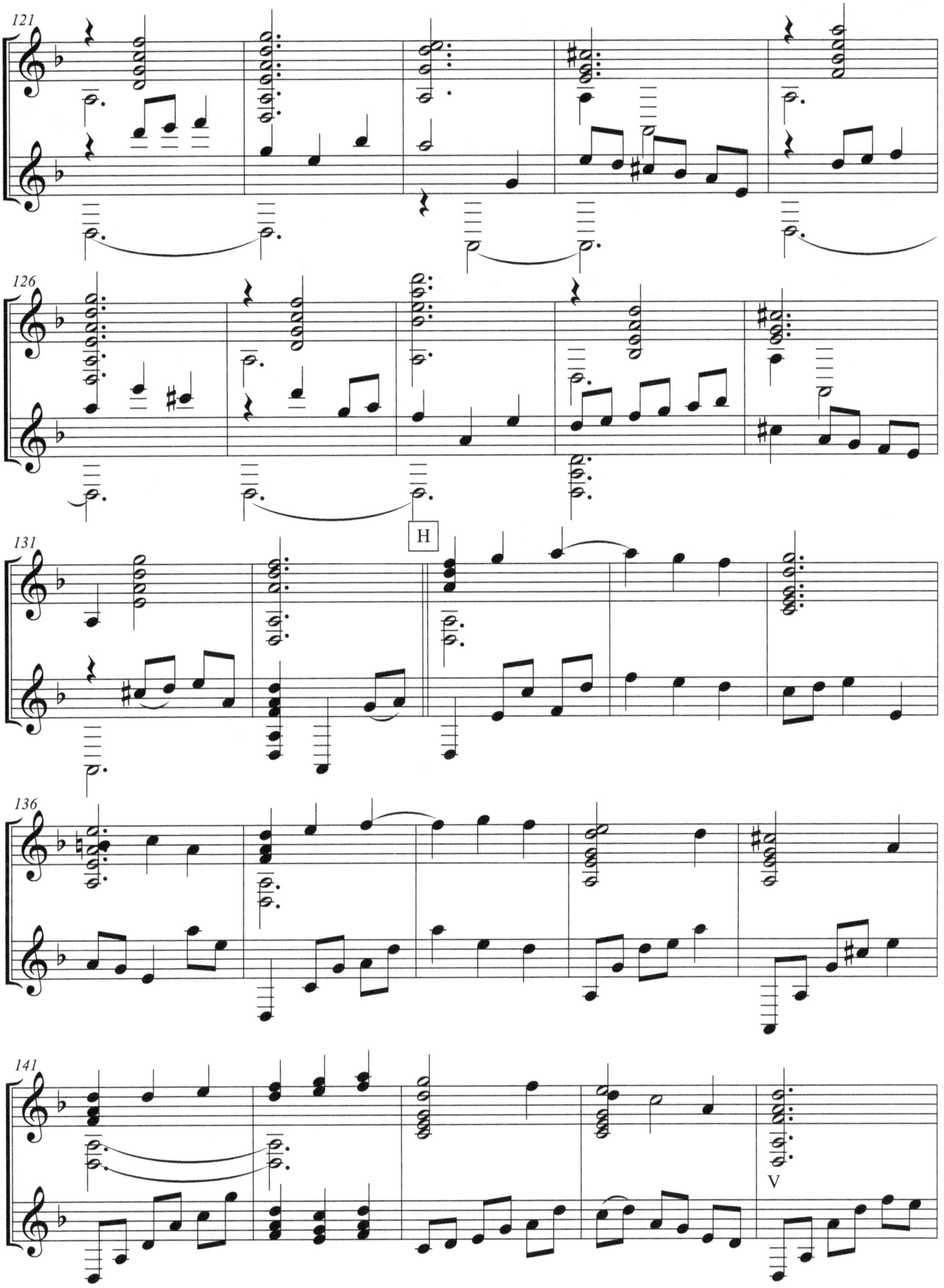
121
126
131
H
136
141
V

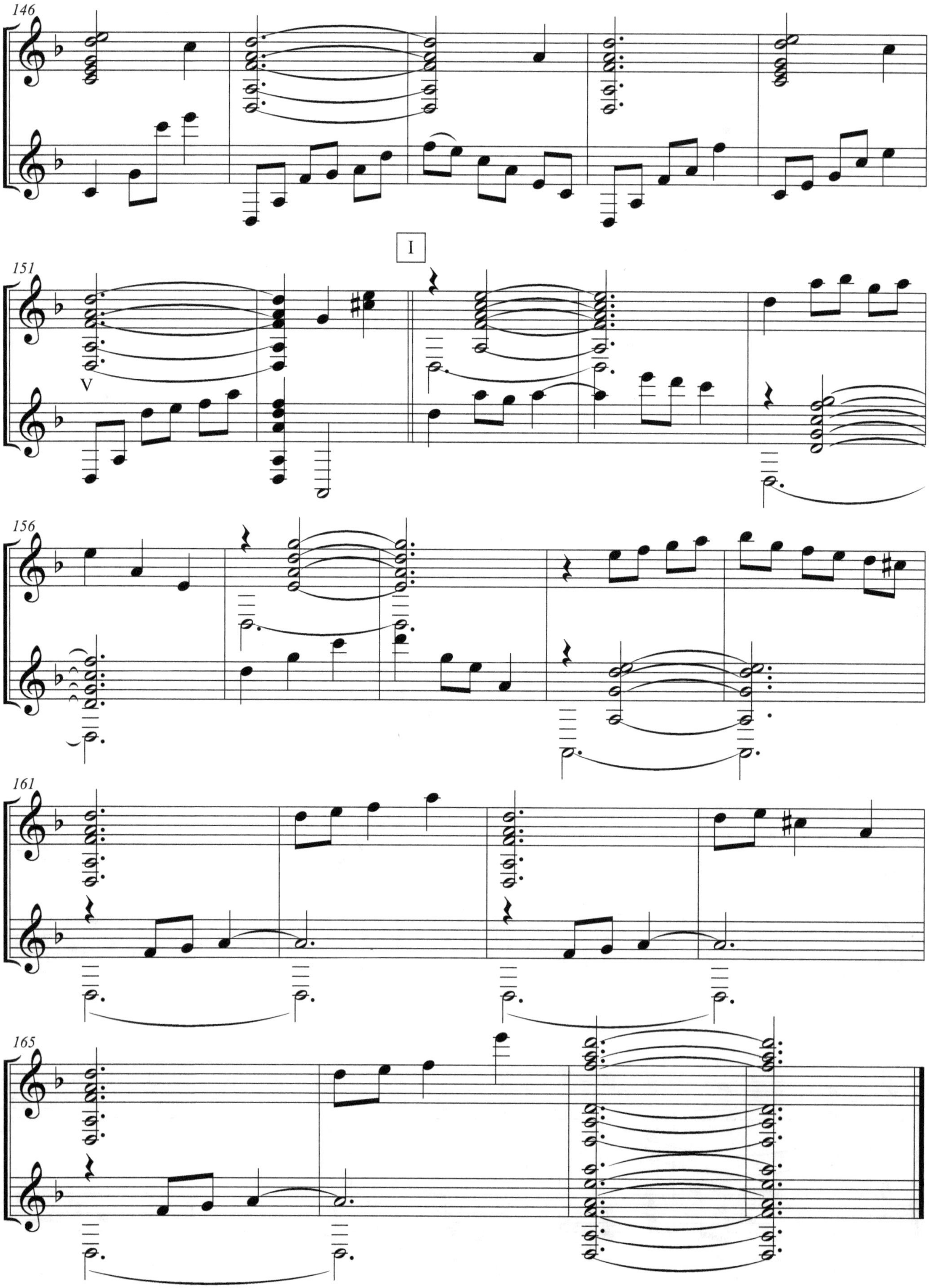
146
151
I
V
156
161
165

This page has been left blank
to avoid awkward page turns.

Fading Dream

William Bay

66

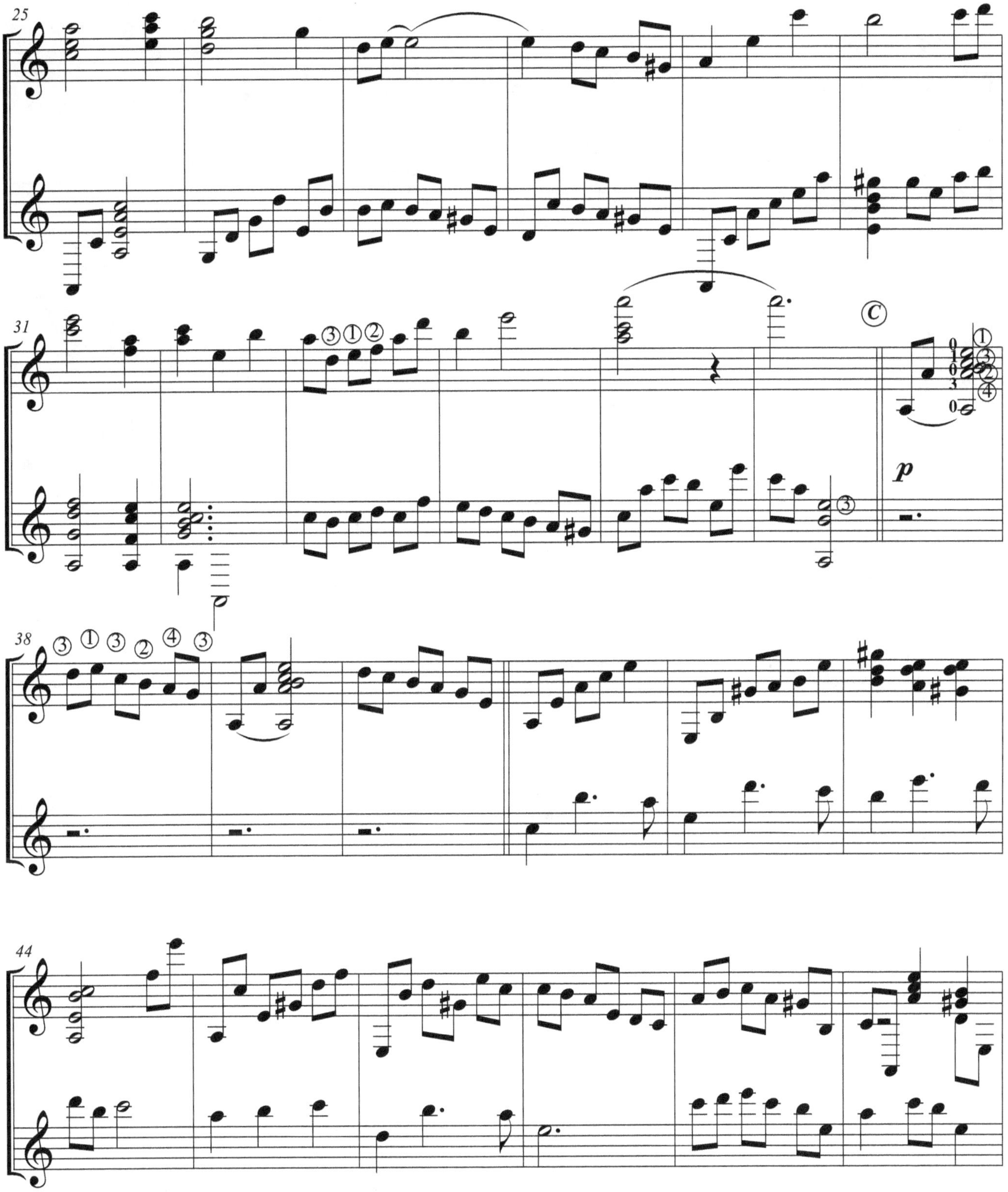
25
31
C
p
38
44

D.C. al Coda

D.C. al Coda

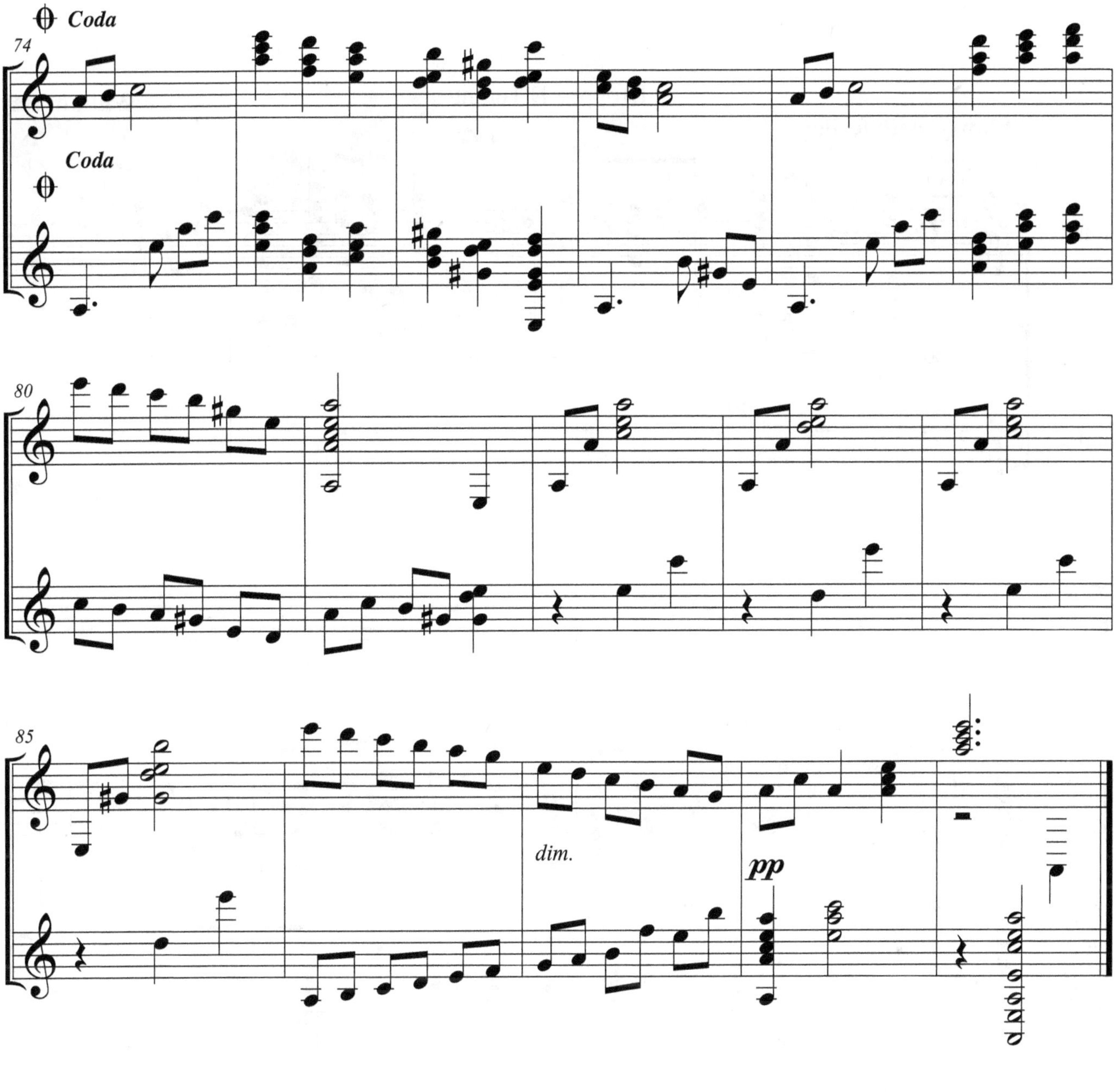
Coda
74
Coda
80
85
dim.
pp

Hymn

Dropped D Tuning

William Bay

Slowly, with feeling

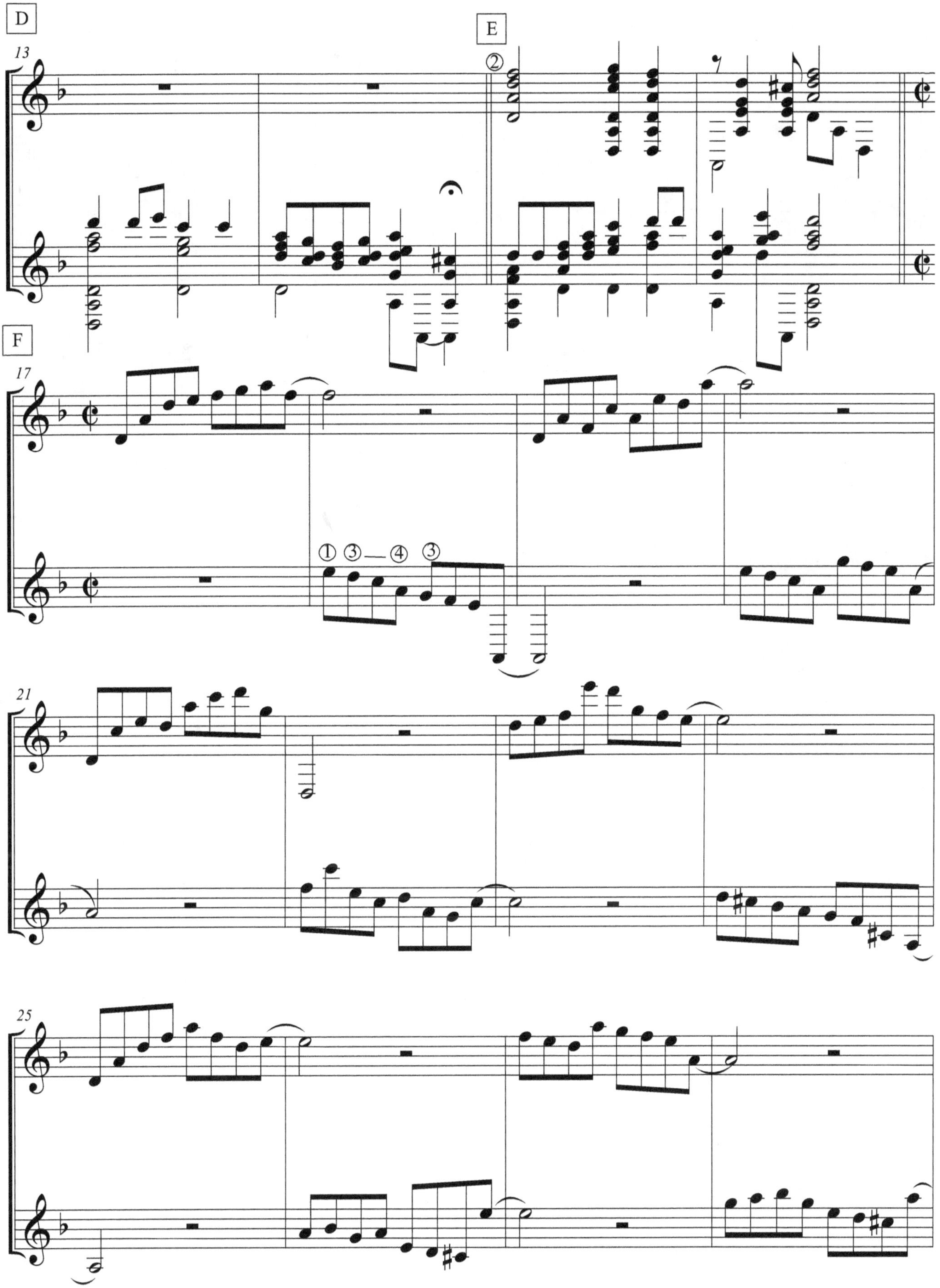
D
13
E
②
F
17
① ③ — ④ ③
21
25

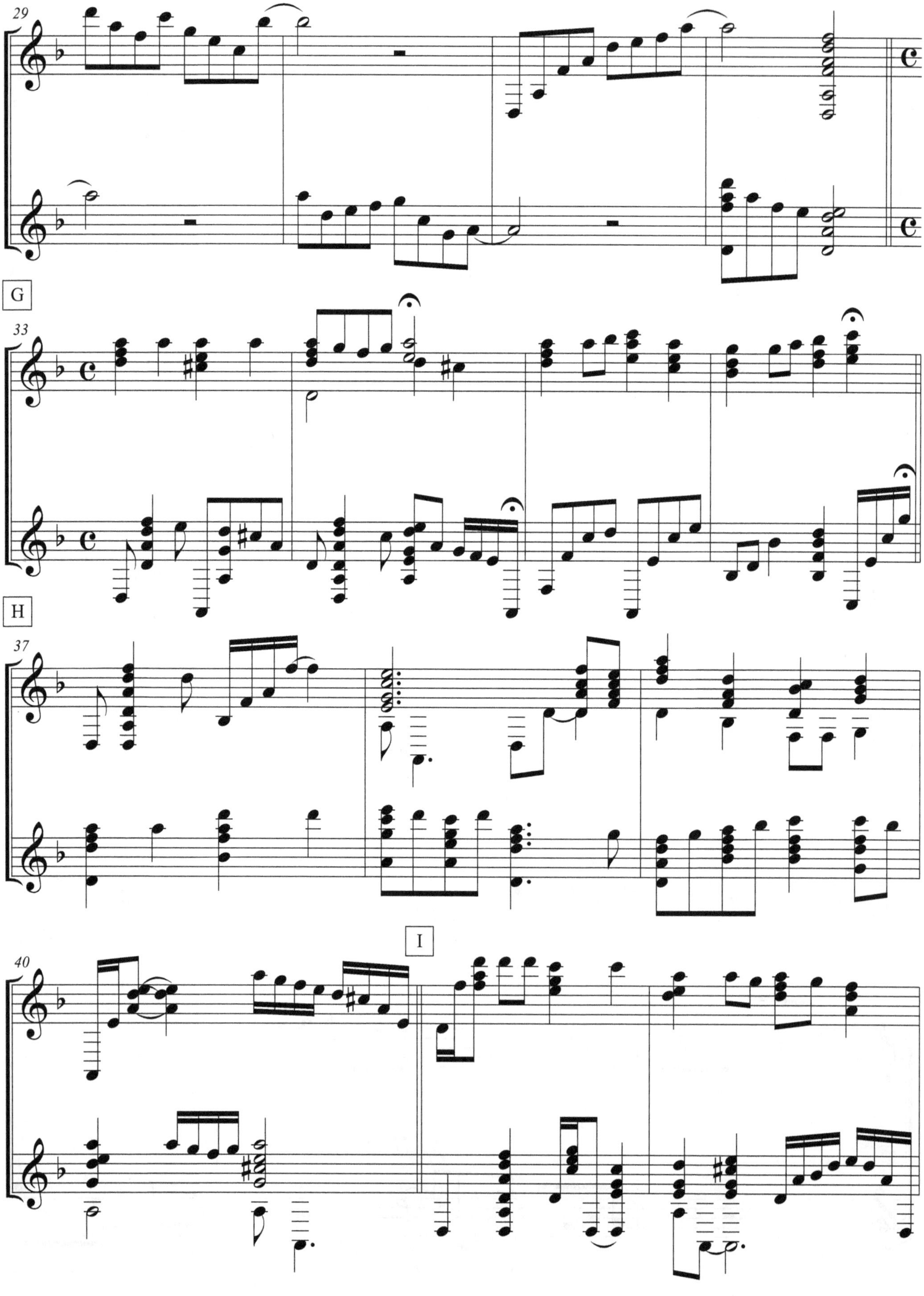
29
G
33
H
37
40
I

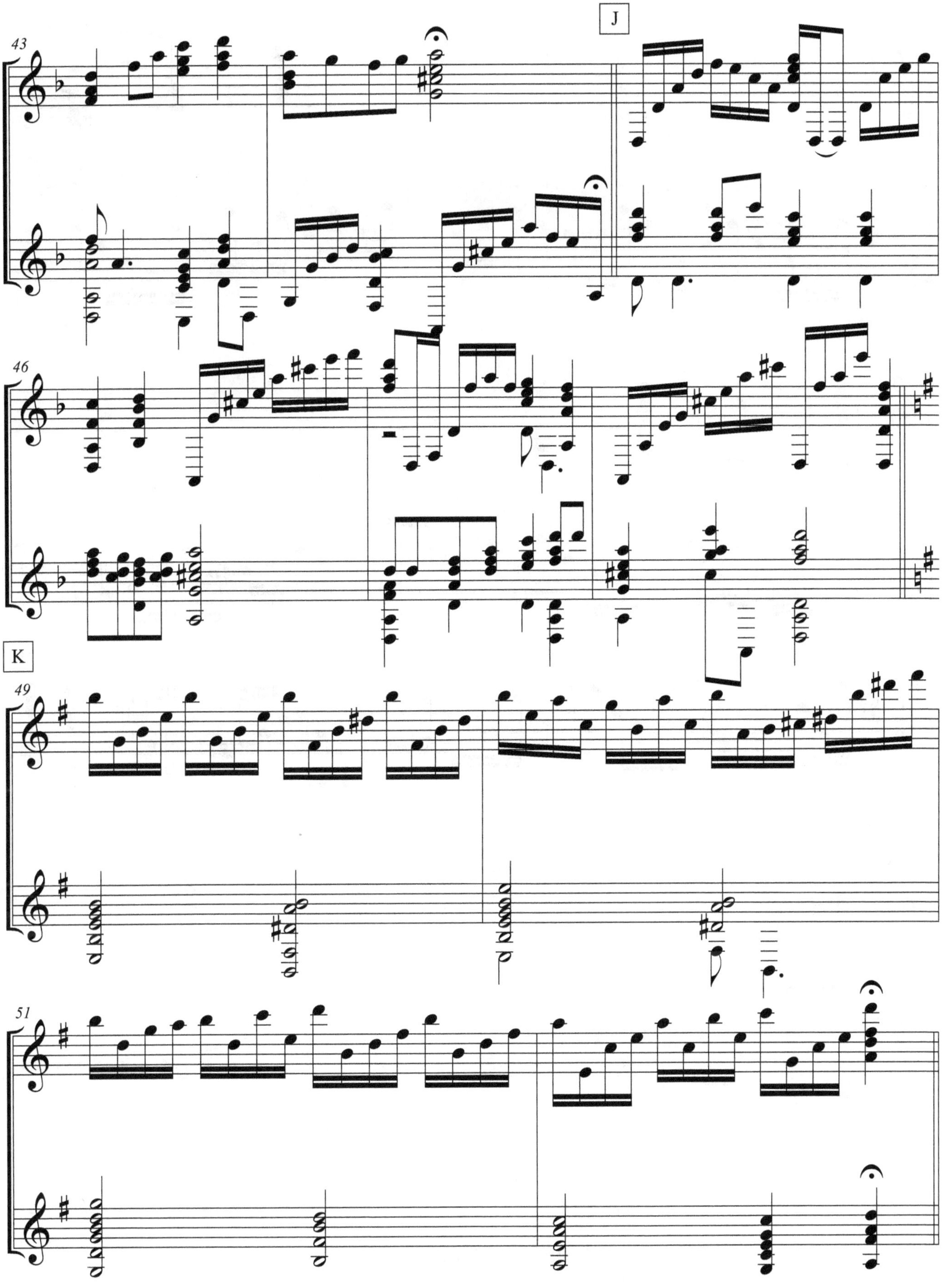
43
J
46
K
49
51

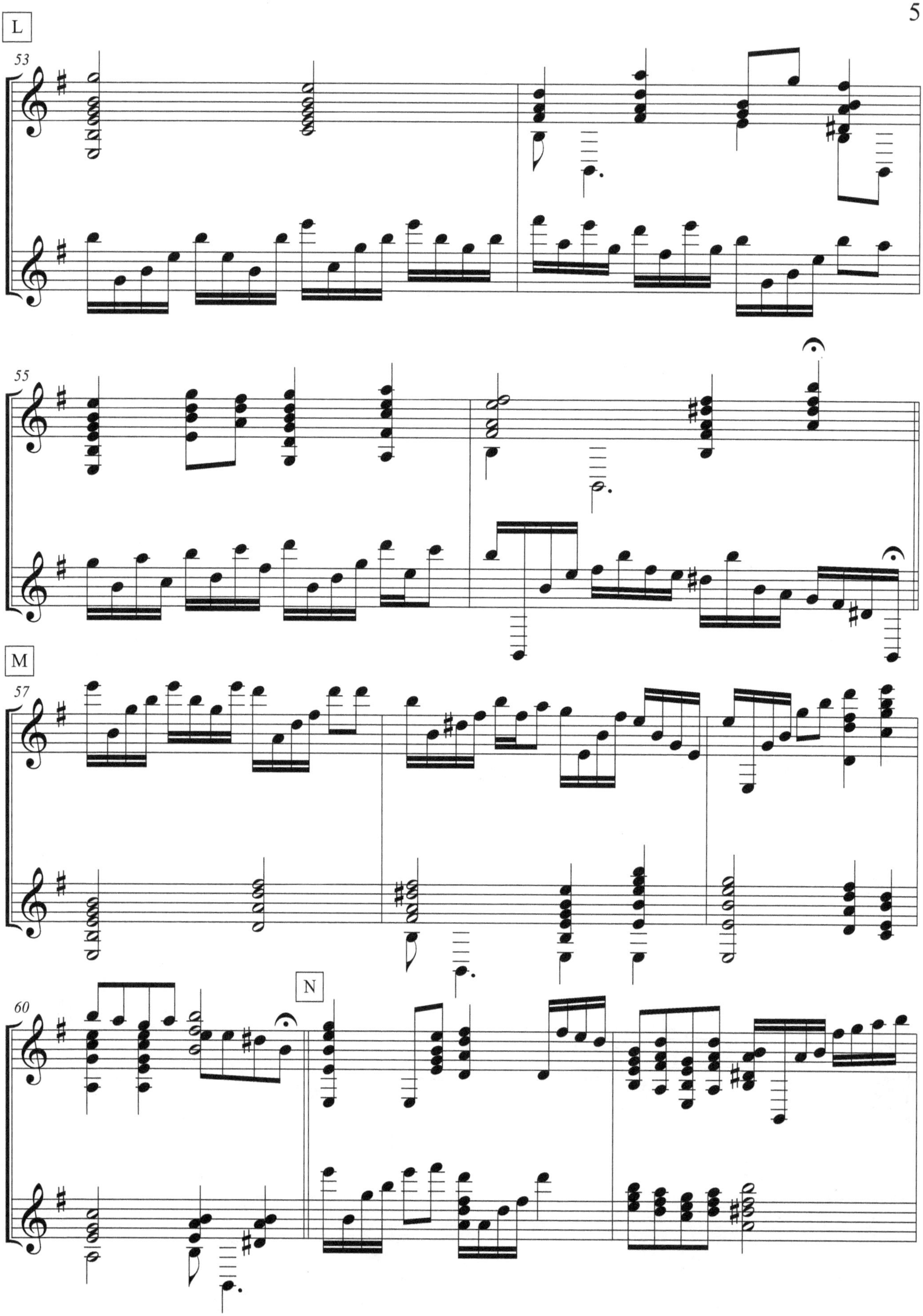
L
53
55
M
57
60
N

Harm. 12

Reflections

William Bay

76

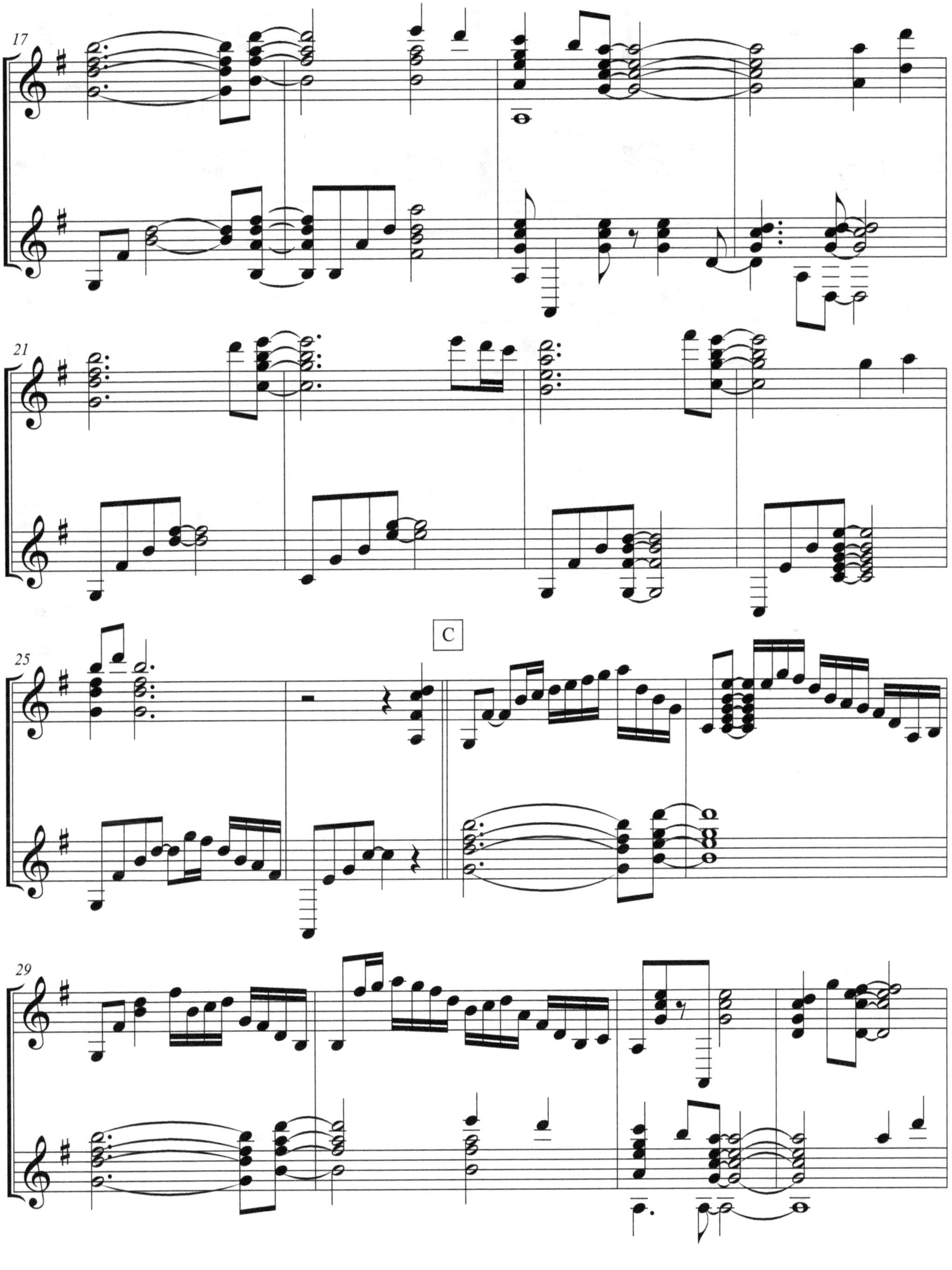
17
21
25
C
29

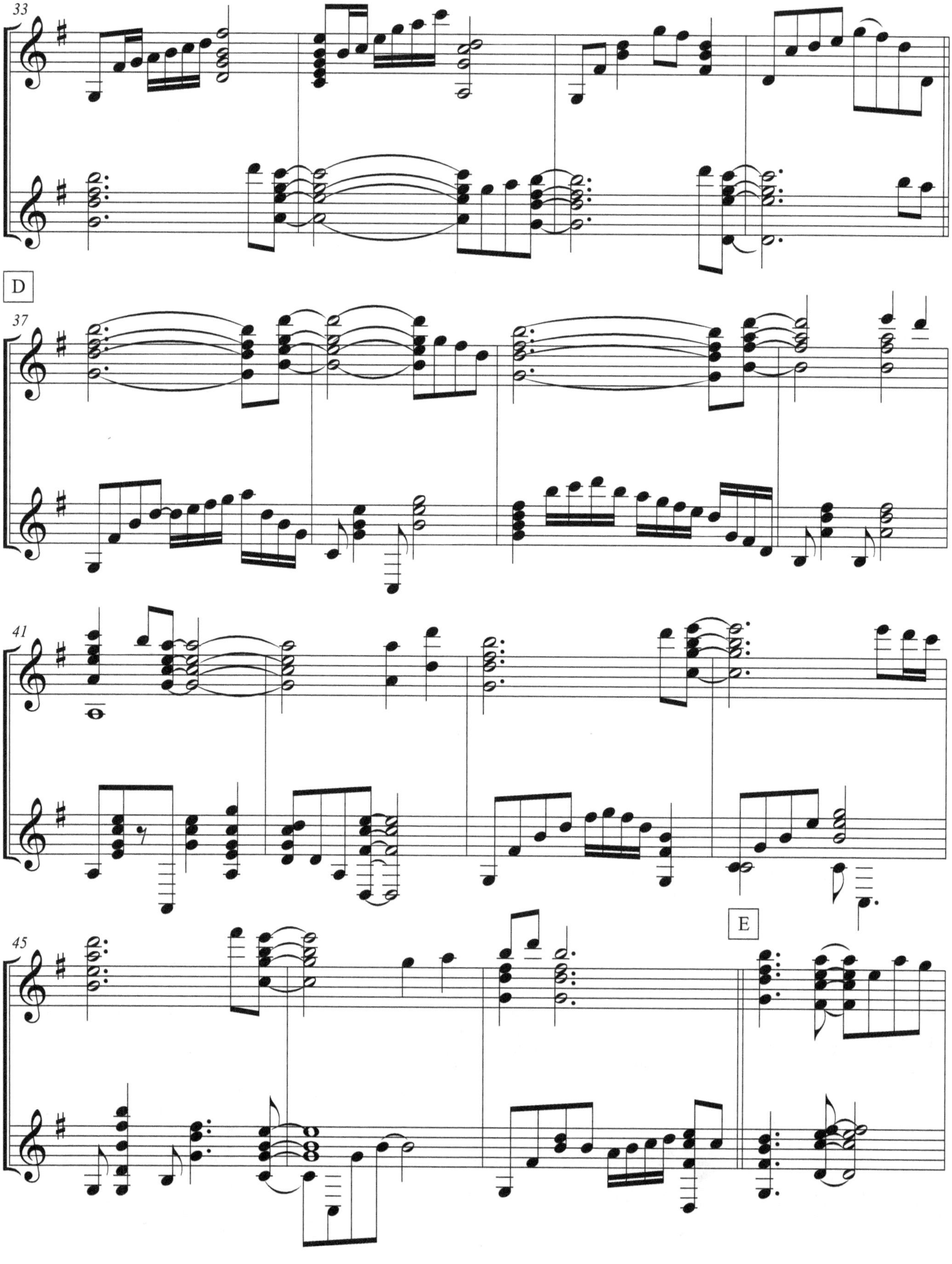
33
D
37
41
E
45

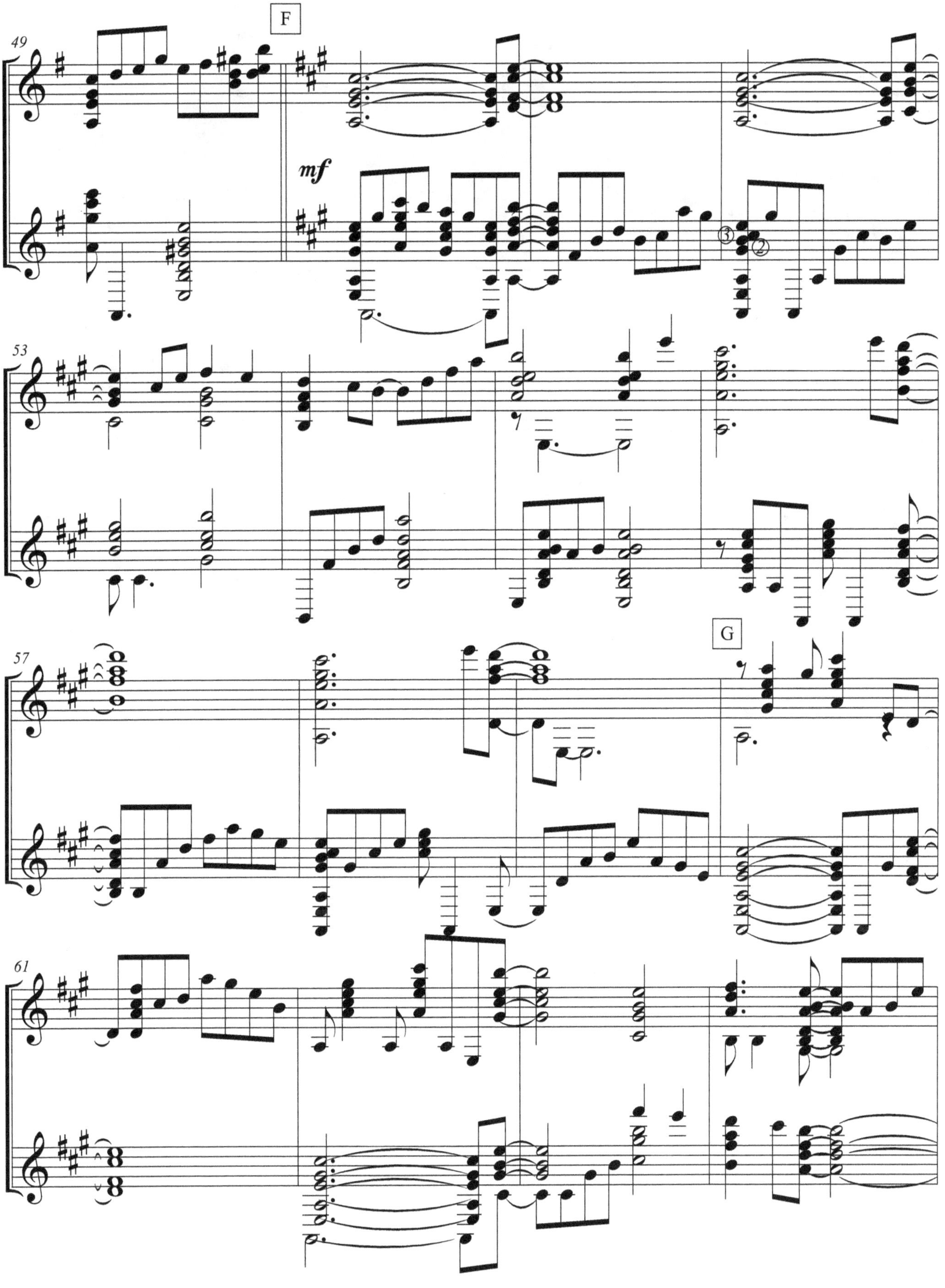
49
F
mf
53
57
G
61

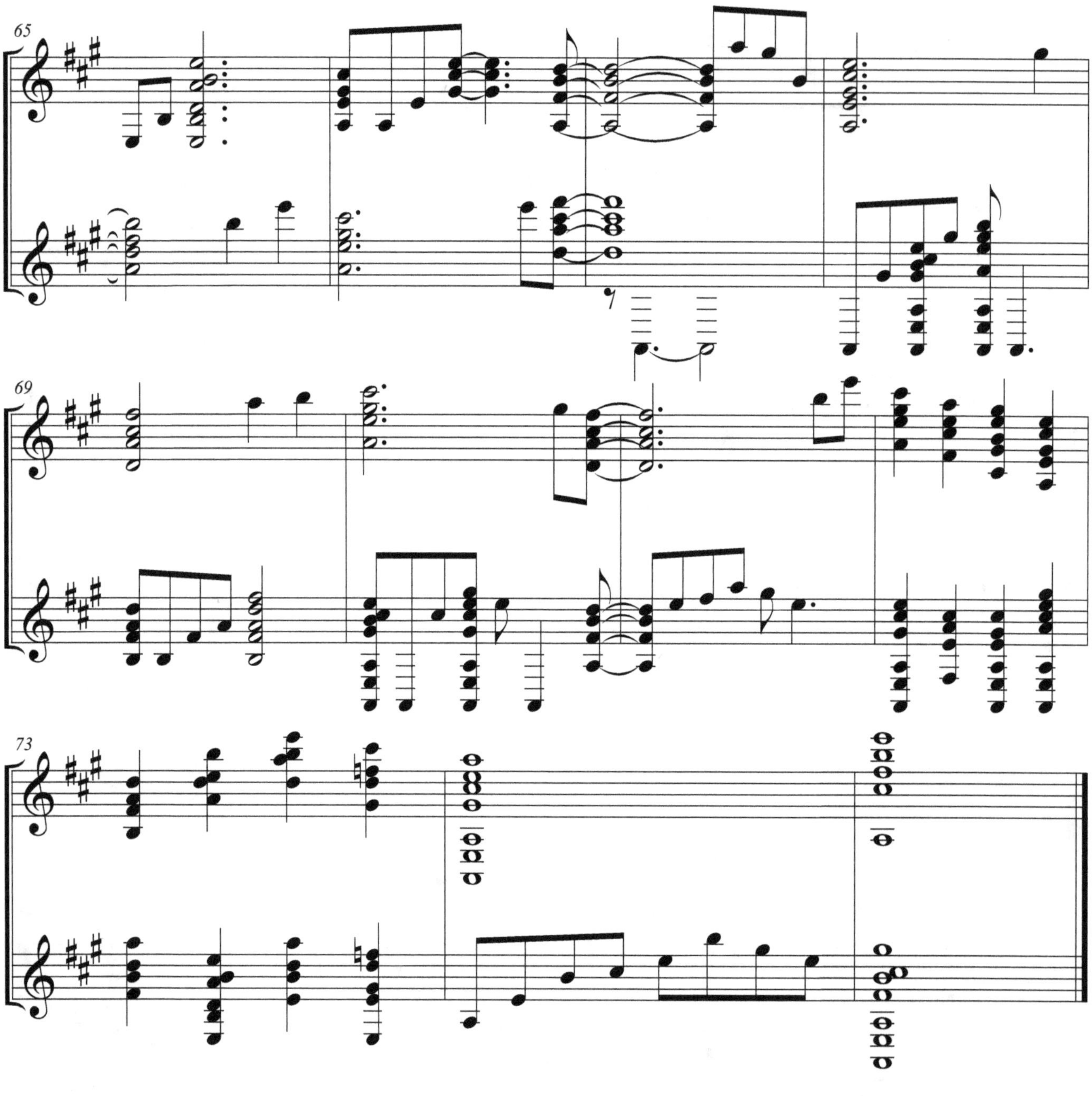
65
69
73

Signals

Allegro ♩. = 96

William Bay

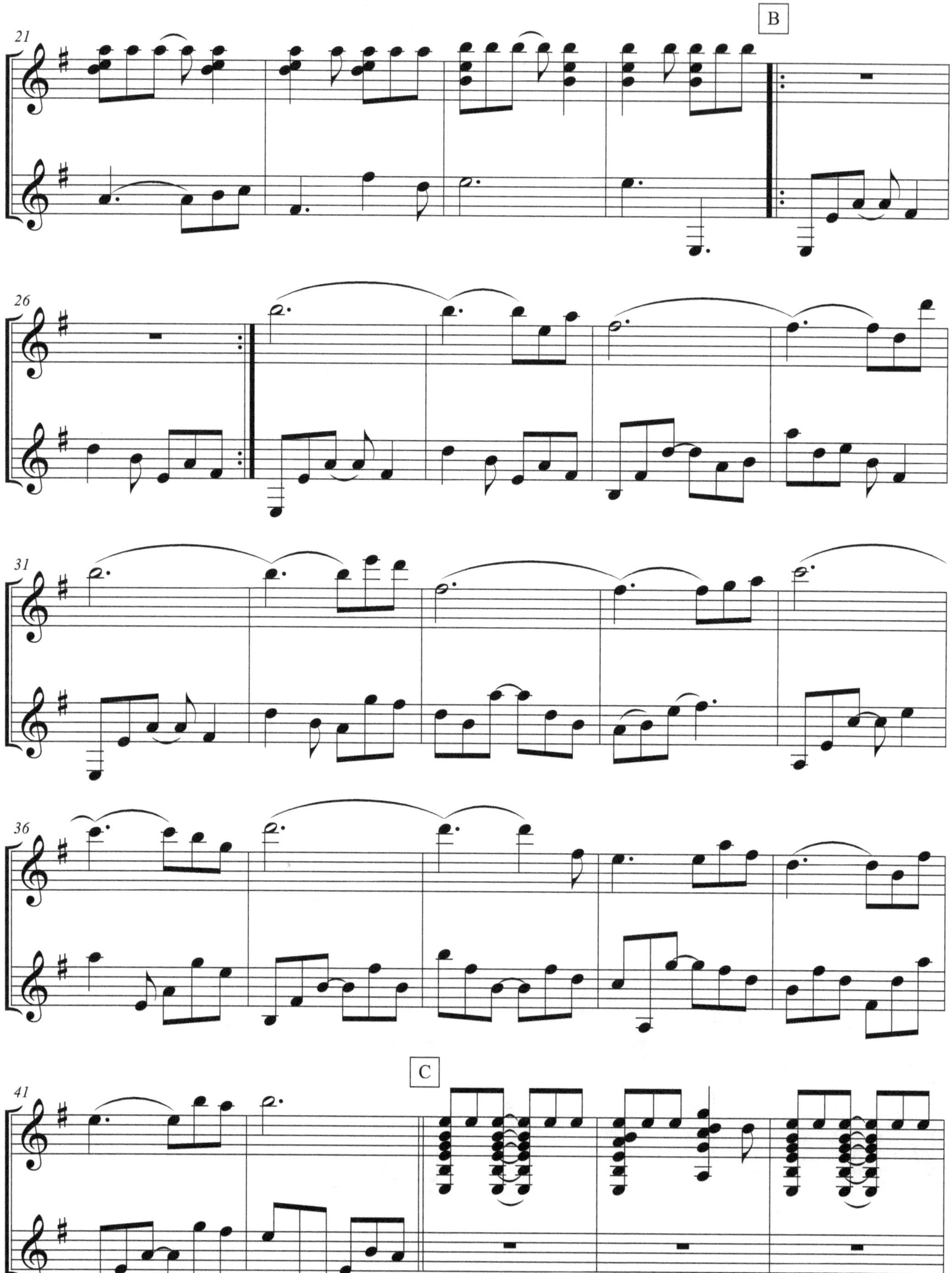

21
B
26
31
36
41
C

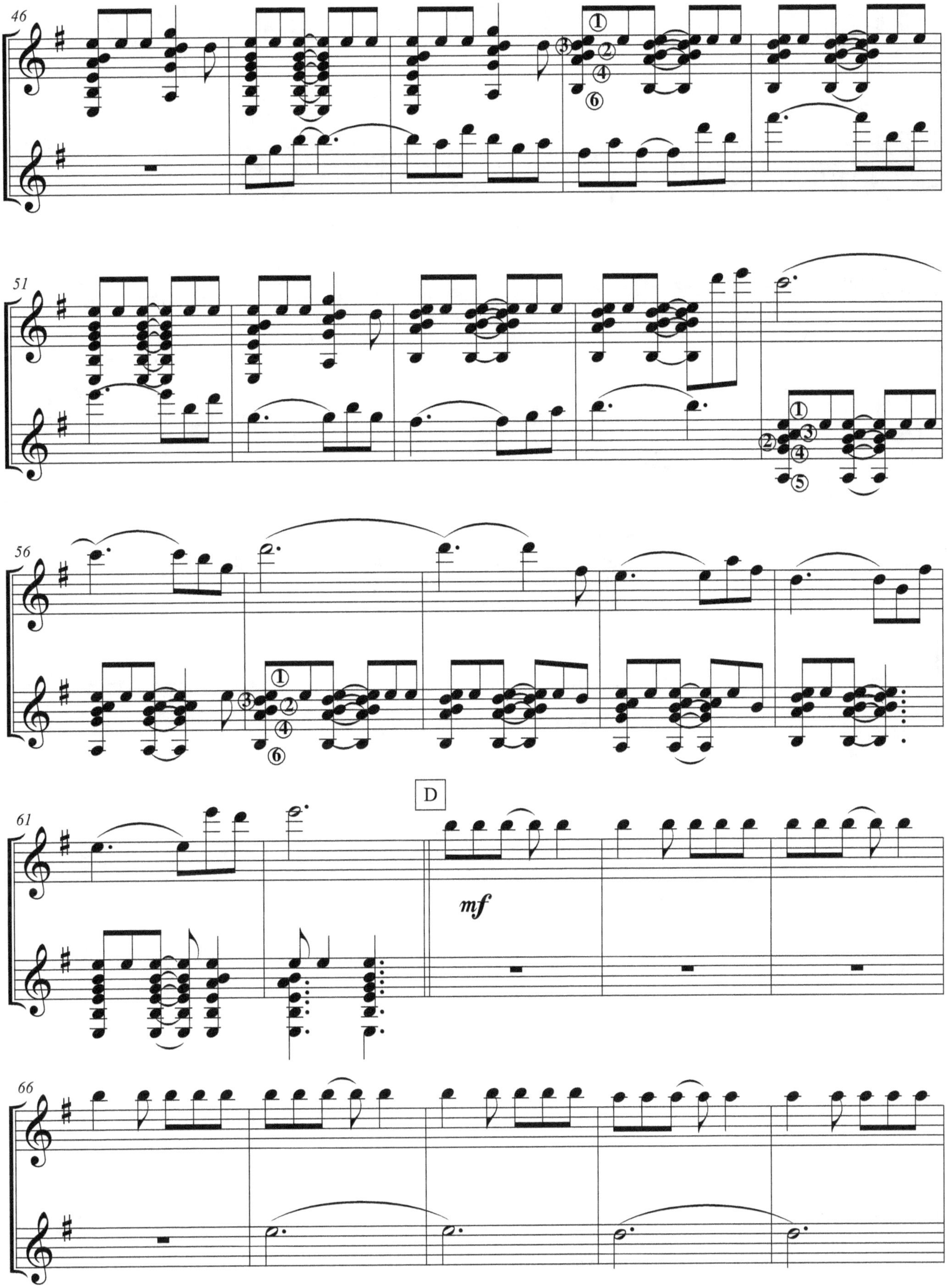
46
51
56
61
D
mf
66

Repeat 4 times

E

Repeat 4 times

2nd time 8va

F

Repeat 5 times   Fade ending

Repeat 5 times | Fade ending

Twilight

⑦= B

Expressively ♩ = 84

William Bay

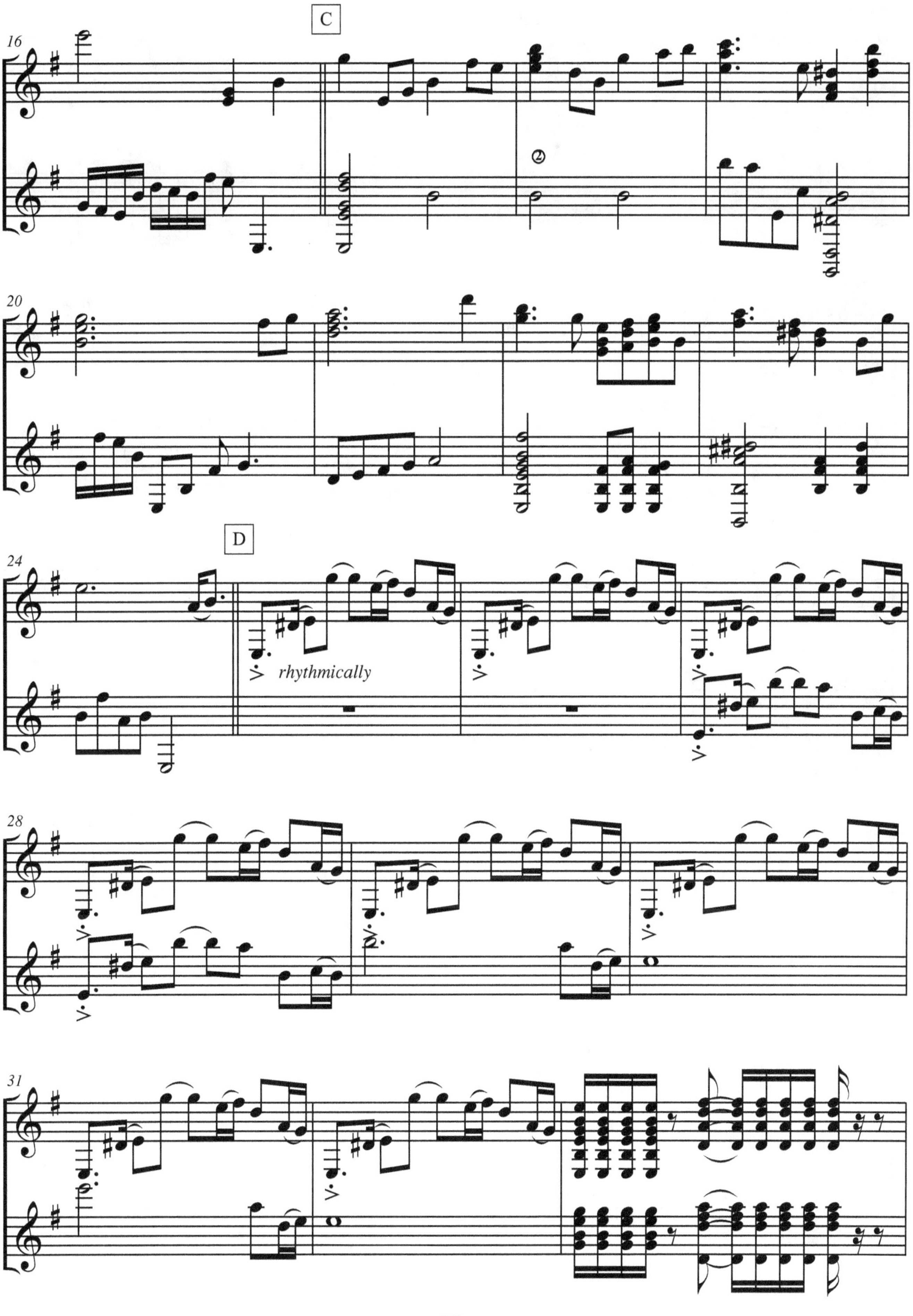
16
C
20
24
D
rhythmically
28
31

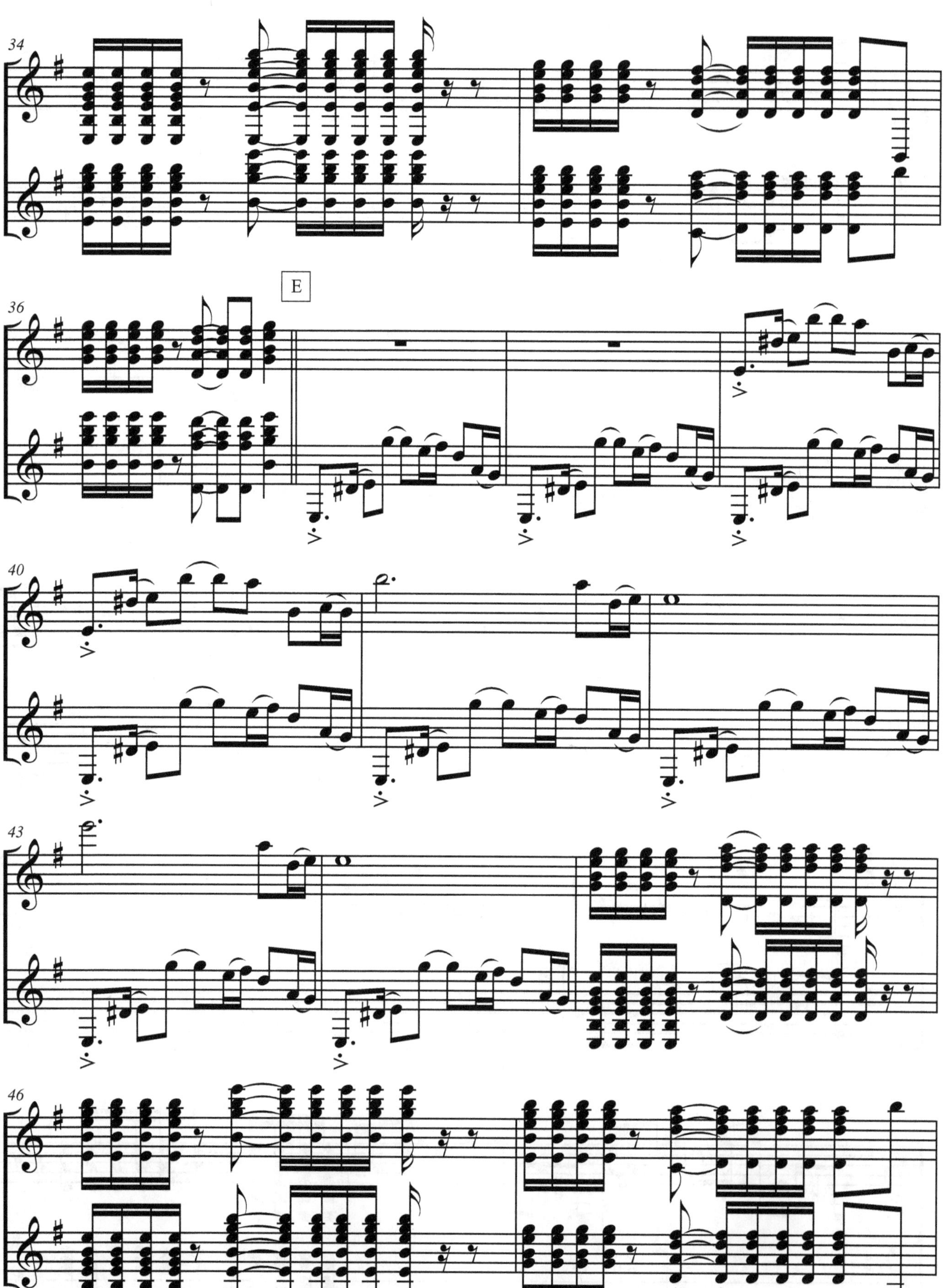
34
36
E
40
43
46

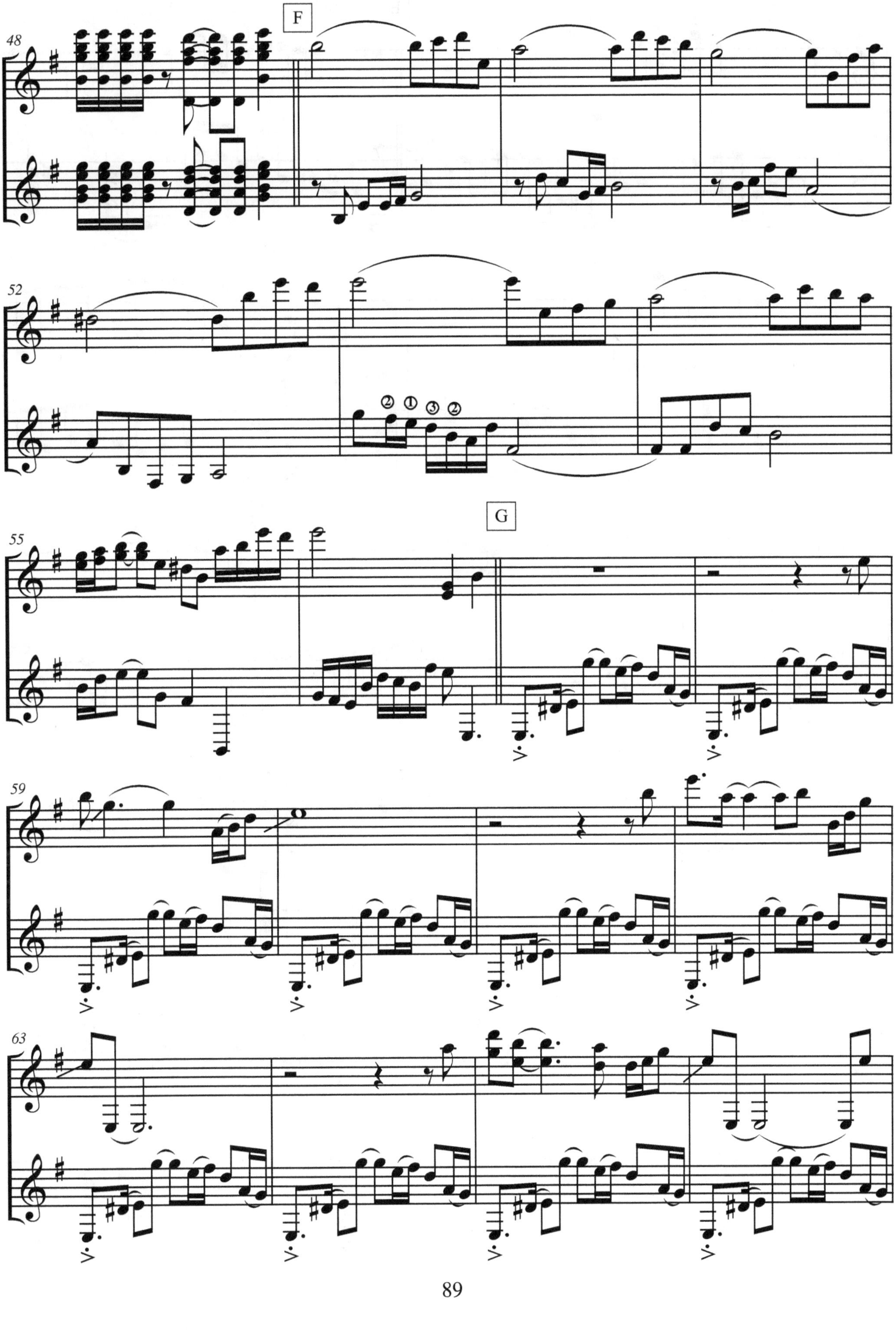
48
F
52
55
G
59
63

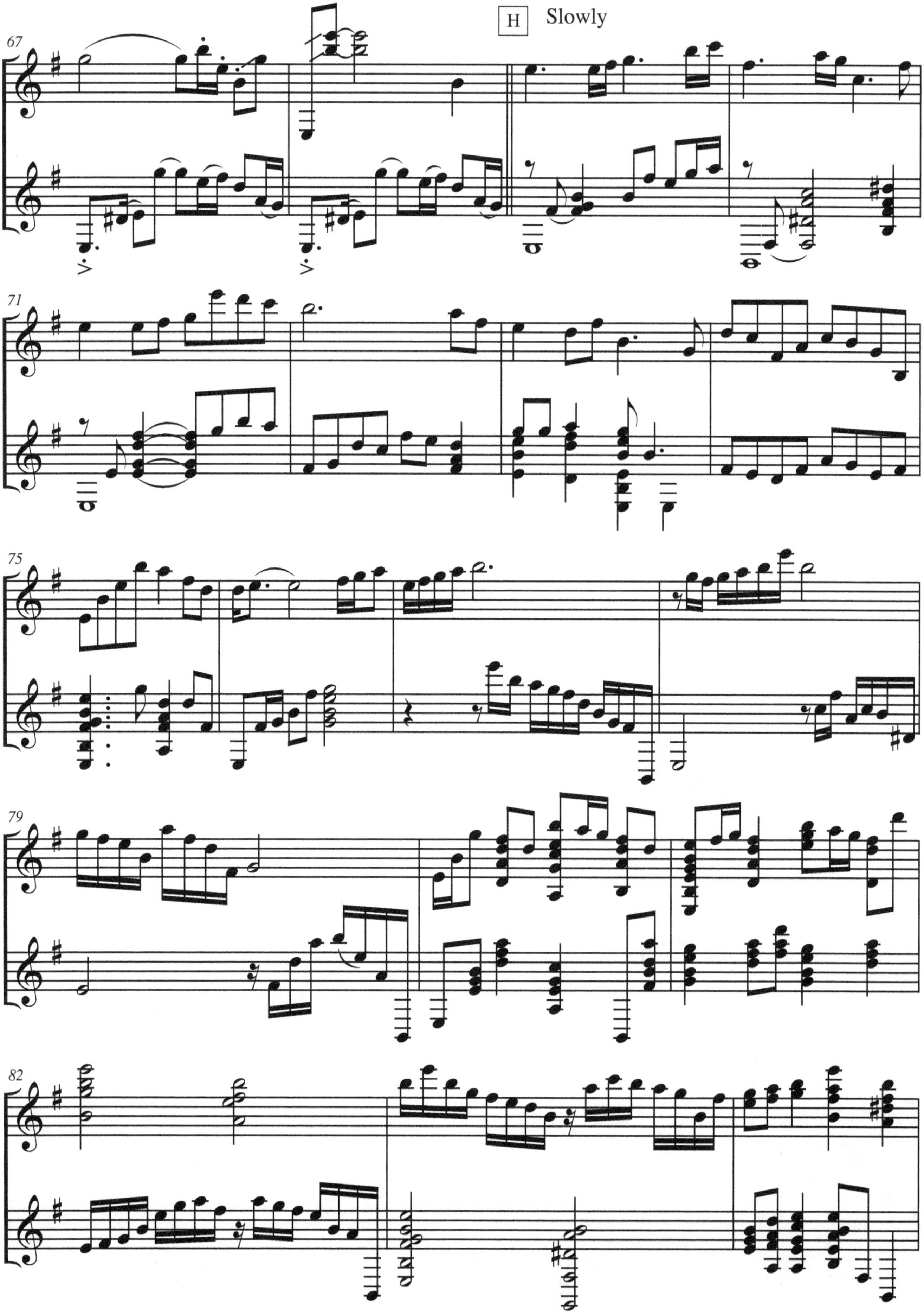
H
Slowly
67
71
75
79
82

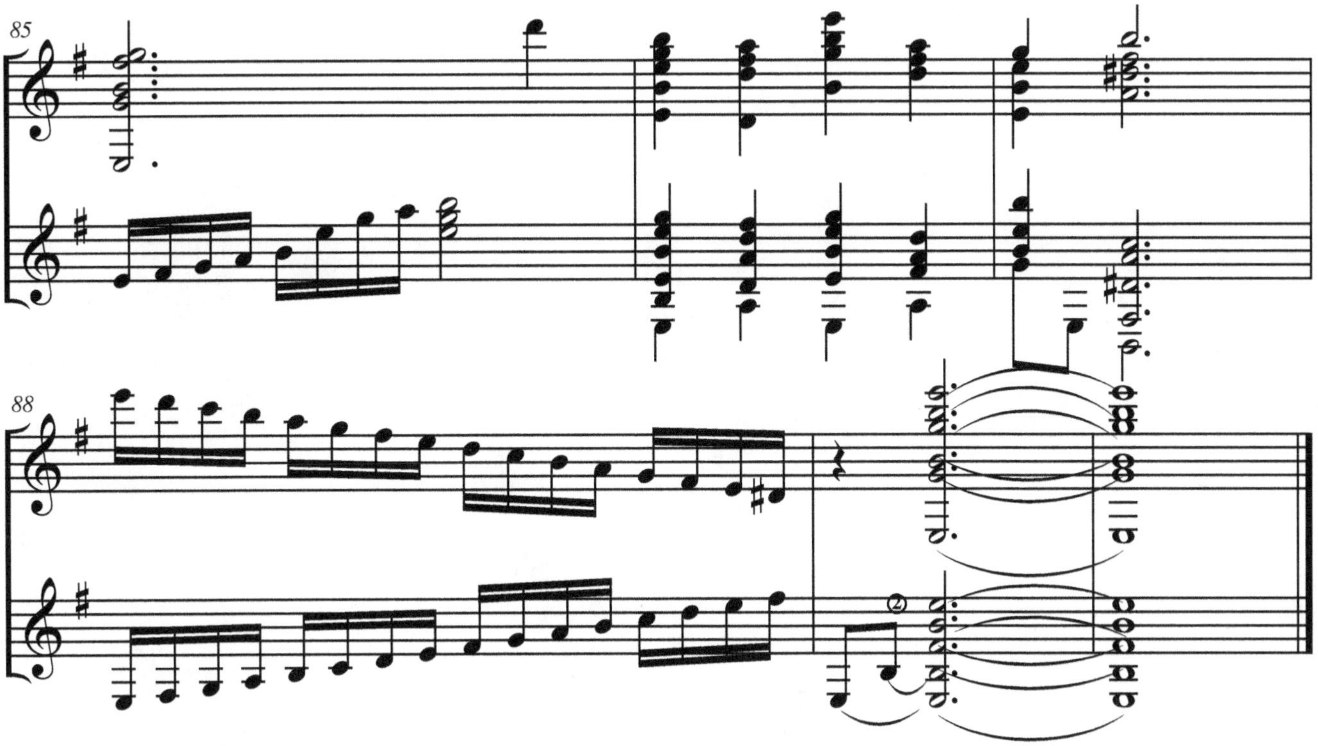
85
88
2

WILLIAM
BAY**MUSIC**

www.ingramcontent.com/pod-product-compliance
Lightning Source LLC
Chambersburg PA
CBHW081436090426
42740CB00017B/3322